MODERN ART OF ASIA
new movements and old traditions

MODERN

by Husain, India

ART OF ASIA

NEW MOVEMENTS AND OLD TRADITIONS

edited by

JAPAN CULTURAL FORUM

Nihon Bunka Fōramu

Published by

TOTO SHUPPAN COMPANY, LIMITED

Tokyo, Japan

Published by
Toto Shuppan Co., Ltd.,
4, 2-chome, Nishi-Kanda,
Chiyoda-ku, Tokyo, Japan

Copyright in Japan, 1961
by Japan Cultural Forum,
11, Shin Ryudo-cho, Azabu,
Minato-ku, Tokyo, Japan

Book design by Yoshihiko Satake
Color plates by Mitsumura Color Plate Printing Co., Ltd., Tokyo
Half-tone plates by Hanshichi Printing Co., Ltd., Tokyo
Letterpress by Chiyoda Publishing & Printing Co., Ltd., Tokyo

Printed and Manufactured in Japan

FOREWORD

In November, 1957, under the auspices of the Japan Cultural Forum, the first Young Asian Artists Exhibition was held in Tokyo. It was decided that, toward furthering international cultural exchange and as a by-product of the exhibition, a history of the art of Asia would be published.

For consultation on the approaching exhibition, I visited Hong Kong, Pakistan, India, Ceylon, Thailand, Singapore, Burma, and Indonesia during the year. In the course of the trip I requested appropriate persons to prepare art histories of the respective countries. Thanks to their enthusiastic cooperation, all the manuscripts were received at about the time of the exhibition. The present book is made up of those manuscripts, plus an art history sent from the Philippines, and one for Japan.

For the fact that, in spite of this fine spirit of cooperation, publication of the volume has been delayed until now, responsibility rests on the Japanese side, and I must apologize to all the contributors. With this publication, however, the plans of the Young Asian Artists Exhibition are completed, and we now have the result of the endeavor to bring together manuscripts by specialists on the art of the various countries of Asia. I believe this book to be of the greatest importance.

In choosing the illustrations, we have attempted to place special emphasis on young, new artists. We regret, however, that limitations of space have forced us to omit many deserving painters.

Mr. Edward Seidensticker has overseen the editing of the English, and I wish here to offer him my most sincere thanks. I wish also to thank our publishers, the Toto Shuppan Company for their generous cooperation.

Takachiyo Uemura
Director, Japan Cultural Forum

January 4, 1961

PURPOSE OF THE EXHIBITION

In November of 1957 the Japan Cultural Forum (affiliated to the international Congress for Cultural Freedom) sponsored the First Exhibition of Young Asian Artists. We feel that confrontation of the works of young artists from all over Asia was an event of unique cultural significance that not only acquainted Asian audiences with work being done in our various countries but also provided the basis for bringing this work to the attention of the entire world.

Since the end of World War II, the awakening of national consciousness, which has characterized all of Asia, has manifested itself in the arts as well as in other spheres of life. At the same time, however, there is, we feel, a spiritual current common to all nations and peoples which manifests itself in similar forms of artistic expression. One of the interesting aspects of the Exhibition was the state of conflict and harmony of the national and the universal trends.

The Exhibition, we feel, not only gave the public a chance to enjoy the newer developments in modern Asian art that we find in the works of younger artists, but also showed that the advancement of forms of artistic expression is in itself proof of the value of artistic freedom.

This First Exhibition is conceived as the beginning of a series to be continued over the years. It is also hoped at some not too distant date to exchange Asian exhibits with France and other countries of the world.

We are pleased to be able to announce that we have received invaluable aid and cooperation from the Yomiuri Newspaper (Tokyo), the International Congress for Cultural Freedom (Paris), the Asian Office of the Congress for Cultural Freedom (New Delhi), the Farfield Foundation (New York), Mr. Julius Fleischmann (Cincinnati), distinguished patron of young artists, and Mr. Donald Stralem (New York), prominent art collector. The Selection Jury had the whole-hearted cooperation of eminent Japanese art critics who assured that the highest possible standards of fairness and of artistic quality prevailed in the determination of awards.

Kenzo Takayanagi
Representative, Japan Cultural Forum
Ichiro Fukuzawa
Exhibition Committee

TABLE OF CONTENTS

LIST OF COLOR PLATES

LIST OF PLATES

ART IN BURMA
by U THEIN HAN

In Burma, today, traditional Burmese art and the latest trends in Western art run in parallel lines, each retaining its own individuality. While Burmese builders still use the traditional style of architecture in pagodas (stupas) and monasteries, functional buildings, such as the new Engineering College, the Technical High School and the Burma Broadcasting Service follow the latest international formula and are welcomed with enthusiasm. Burmese sculptors are still making polished images of Buddha in the conventional style; and the portrait statue of Bogyoke Aung San, the liberator of Burma, in the rough medium of bronze, was at first hard to stomach but is now accepted by the Rangoon public without protest. While the majority of Burmese painters are still illustrating scenes from the life of Buddha and the Jataka stories for the benefit of religious donors, some make audacious attempts at modern abstract art in frescoes and popular magazines.

The situation may seem baffling, but it is only a repetition of experiences that prevailed Burmese art from the 11th century to the end of the 19th, and it is expected eventually to bring a fusion of the two main currents into one, which can be called a new Burmese art. The only problem to-day is how to avoid the production of bastard art and how to build up a harmonious blend of the two, for classical Burmese Art emerged out of a successful fusing of indigenous art with the Buddhist art of Peninsular India of the 8th and 9th centuries.

2

We do not know the nature of the indigenous art. When the early ancestors of modern Burmans, having descended from the plains of Central Asia through Southwestern China, settled in the plains of Burma, however,

they already had an animistic cult, the peculiar social customs and institutions of Central Asian tribes, and above all a knowledge of Chinese culture.

First, they founded two tribal states, Srikestra (old Prome) and Thaton—
the former on the Irrawaddy river and the latter on the Gulf of Martaban.
From the 5th century A.D., a relationship was established with the states of
Peninsular India. Of all the Indian influences, Thera-vada Buddhism was
the strongest, and when both Srikestra and Thaton adopted Thera-vada
Buddhism for their state religion, Indo-Buddhist art, the handmaid of
Buddhism, was also bound to be accepted in the new land. Burmese art
then began its brilliant career and gradually developed, as in the other
countries of Southeast Asia, towards the emergence of a classical national
art.

Srikestra flourished for 300 years and then perished, while Thaton lived
longer but became weak towards the end of the 10th century. However,
before the close of the 10th century the new land was dotted with numerous
stupas and temples. The stupas of Baw Baw and Be-be and the temples of
Lemyet-na and Zegu can still be seen in the deserted walled city of old
Prome and the stupas of Shwe-za-yan and Thagya-paya still stand in modern
Thaton.

In the 11th century a powerful new kingdom, Pagan, arose in Middle
Burma under the leadership of Anawrahta. He was the first monarch to
unify the petty states into one political and cultural unit. He conquered
Thaton and expanded his territory down to Mergui in the south and up to
Mytikyina in the north. He made the city of Pagan the seat of Buddhist
culture, building the first national library of Buddhist scriptures and con-
structing the beautiful stupas of Shwe-zan-daw and Shwe-zi-gon at the capital.
Then he opened his empire to the outer world, particularly to India.

During his reign, national consciousness and religious zeal were such
that he succeeded in paving the way for prodigious architectural and artistic
activities down to destruction of Pagan by Kublai Khan in the 13th century.

For two hundred years after Anawrahta, Pagan, faithful to the policy
of her founder, erected numerous stupas and temples in various architectural
styles and accumulated thousands of sculptures and wall-paintings. Today
within a five-mile radius of old Pagan there can still be seen nearly five
thousand religious monuments of various shapes and sizes, those that survived
the ravages of war, weather, and time. Among them one can easily pick
out the stupas of Shwe-zi-gon and Mingala-zedi and the temples of Ananda
and Thabyin-nyu for their architectural styles; Nan-paya and Pet-leik for their
sculptures; and Nanda-minnya and Paya-Thonzu for their wall-paintings.
They became models for architects and artists of succeeding generations.

3

In India, Buddhism from the time of Asoka became the source of
inspiration for artistic activities, and produced a specific school of art and
architecture. Buddhist stupas, monasteries, temples and images had system-
atized forms and types. There were fixed rules for the iconography, prescribed

symbols and gestures, and various art styles, such as Barhut, Mathura, Sanchi, Amaravati, Ghandara, Gupta and Pala. Before the school of art and architecture known as Indo-Buddhist spread to Southeast Asia, it had already reached its highest development. When Buddhism came to Burma, Indo-Buddhist art undoubtedly helped to propagate the faith in the new land. As it was a popular art, it easily gained a warm place in the heart of the people, and later it came to be practised by native artists.

It is obvious now that the classical art of Burma was basically of Indian origin and that its purpose was, as in India, mainly religious and ethical. However, it seems that classical Burmese art had not lost contact with the genius of indigenous art, simple and crude though the latter might be. No doubt it adopted Indian forms and types, observed Indian symbols and iconography, and followed Indian models, but it was not entirely imitative. Considering the un-Indian appearances of the Pagan stupas and temples, one can safely say that classical Burmese art successfully assimilated the two elements—foreign and native, profound and simple.

Of the two kinds of buildings, stupa and temple, which formed the largest number of religious monuments in Burma, the Burmese stupa is a typical example of the Burmese version of an Indian original. The stupa in India and Ceylon was essentially a reliquary built in the form of a hemispherical dome, suggestive of a sacred burial mound. When the Burmans started building their stupas in Srikestra and later in Pagan, they broadened the base, and reduced the bulbous mass to such a size that the suggestion changed from the idea of a burial mound to that of Mount Meru, the abode of celestial beings—the abode surmounted by Nirvana. They built at the base three or five receding terraces and placed on it an octagon, then a bell, then rings, then a group made up of inverted lotus and balls and open lotus, then a plantain bud, and finally an umbrella. This was surely a new design to produce a soaring effect. The Burmese stupa achieved a perfect balance between the convexity of an Indian stupa and the concavity of a Chinese pagoda. The Shwe-zigon of Pagan and the Shwedagon of Rangoon (*Color Pl. 1*) are typical examples of this new Burmese design.

In temple architecture there is no place to rival old Pagan in Burma. The great temples of Ananda and Thabyinnyu and the small temples of Nan-paya and Nanda-mannya are still well preserved and tended. The purpose of the temple was as in India to enshrine the image of Buddha. It was rectangular or square in plan with one projecting portico or four. Its roof rose above the central chapel in the form of a stupa. The design was, like the stupa, intended to convey emotions of elevation and reverence. Inside the temple, however, the change was abrupt. The pointed arches and the groined ceiling, the narrow corridor and its half-vault, the small window-apertures and the bareness of the walls, and the high image-chamber and the colossal image in the dim light—all these features produced an effect of religious awe and humility. The Ananda temple by King Kyanzittha should serve as a typical example. Later the building art of Pagan underwent a remarkable change which rejected projecting porticoes and admitted more light and air into the image-chamber.

The stupas and the temples were mainly of brick and stucco, whereas the monasteries and the royal residences were wooden buildings. The latter two classes are considered closer to domestic architecture. One feature common to both was that they were usually built on long posts, covered by multiple-roofs, and provided with wide verandas. The plan of the old city of Mandalay, surrounded by a wall and moat, with the royal palace in the centre, is said to be Pan-Asian and is reminiscent of Marco Polo's description of Kublai Khan's Peking.

4

Compared with architecture, Burmese sculpture and painting did not call for the highest talent in Burmese artists, but curiously enough they won the heart of Burmans, both high and low. So much so that at one time they even became folk arts. Even in a humble village one could without much difficulty find a wood-carver to decorate a religious shrine.

Classical Burmese sculpture and painting have the same story to tell. They were, as in India, more concerned with what the spirit of the artist contemplated than what he actually saw. Inner vision rather than visible appearance was the criterion of expression. They narrated, as in India, famous scenes from the life of Buddha and the Jataka stories. Their chief characteristics were, as in India, iconographic accuracy, symbolic gestures, and a variety of ornamental flower and animal motifs. But Indo-Buddhist influence lingered only through the Pagan period, after which it withdrew gracefully, allowing these two arts the independence of their own national ways.

The majority of the classical sculptures were executed in wood and brick, and the rest in terracotta, bronze, and stone. Most of them were carved or modelled as bas-reliefs and very few as figures in the round. Of all the sculptures the images of Buddha were most numerous. They appeared and reappeared in all mediums and sizes and in different postures of sitting, standing, and reclining. The conventional attitude (Bhumi-pasa mudra, i.e., earth touching) of the seated Buddha with the right hand on the right knee and with the fingers pointing to the earth to prove to Mara, His arch-enemy, the achievements of his previous incarnations at the time of his enlightenment under the Bo tree, was and is still a favourite mudra. The four colossal standing Buddhas, in wood, of the Ananda temple (Pagan), the seated Buddha in bronze of the Maha-Myat-Muni temple (Mandalay), and the reclining Buddha in brick and plaster of the Shwe-tha-yaung temple (Pegu) are accomplished works of art. The stone portraits of King Kyanzittha, the founder of the Ananda temple, and of Shin Arahan, the Buddhist Primate of Pagan, are unique in the history of Burmese sculpture in the sense that the artist consulted life.

The life of Buddha and the Jataka stories were artistically narrated in the stone bas-reliefs of the Ananda, in the terracotta plaques of the Petleik (Pagan), and in the wood-carvings of the Shwedagon (Rangoon) and of the Thein-go-shin (Pakkoku). Ornamental flower and animal motifs (" Chu " or " Kanot ") in all mediums were universal: the gateways, the archways, the pediments, the horn-like gable-ends, the pilasters, the panels, the parapets, the friezes, and the cornices were always lively with the rhythmic movements of lilies and lotuses, vines and orchids, Chinthes (mythical lions), dragons, Kinnaras (Human-birds), yogis, Kitti-mukha (demon-mask) ogres, monkeys, Garudas (mythical birds), Hamsa birds, peacocks, parrots, and the like.

The medium of classical Burmese painting was tempera. Almost all the plastered walls of the temples which sprang up in Upper Burma were adorned with mural paintings. It seems that there was in the beginning a close parallel between sculpture and painting, though naturally they differed in technique. The treatment was such that the figures and the elements of nature appeared as they usually did in sculptures. The chief merit of classical Burmese painting lies in the movement of line. Of the wall-paintings of Pagan, those in the temples of Nanda-mannya, Paya-thonzu, Thambula, and the cave of Kyanzittha Onmin still remain clear and bright. In these structures, there can be seen, in addition to the religious subjects, a lady with her water-goblet, a proud Pagan prince on his horse, a procession of dancing girls, a Mongol commander with his falcon, and a Mongol archer with his bow and arrow. Surely they tell the story of the rise and fall of Pagan. It is now known that in the post-Pagan period the kings of Burma kept painters in the service of the Crown. The Court painters taught religious and moral lessons to the royal children with the help of art. Their other function was the (Parabaik) scroll-painting of the State and ceremonial activities of royalty.

5

The art of modern Burma is modern art. Since the British occupation in 1886, Burma has been opened to the world and western influence has crept into the artistic life of the Burmese nation. The Anglo-Indian architecture of the Secretariat, the High Court, the Law Court, and the Governor's Residence in Rangoon held an eminent position. The only exception was the decoration in classical Burmese style of the City Hall, a reflection of the Burmese national movement for independence. On the other hand new techniques and a new outlook were gained by Burmese painters and sculptors. U Ba Zaw and U Ba Nyan Pl. came back from Europe and founded a school of Western painting. The former was a landscapist in water-colour, while the latter was a portraitist in oil. In sculpture, naturalism found favour with wood-carvers. Today these tendencies continue to work in the Republic of Burma.

ART IN CEYLON

a brief survey of the past and the contemporary
by L. P. GOONETILLEKE

Let me say straightaway that what follows is not a history of art in Ceylon, as was suggested to me; a history is indeed a matter for far more study and research than the writer has been able to undertake, and covers many more fields than can be brought within the scope of a brief article: and, like a well-known Colombo journalist, the author of the latest book on the story of Sinhalese painting just published, I must hasten to say that these are "random jottings" on a vast subject which still requires the attention of scholars; but on the occasion of an International exhibition of paintings by "Young Asian Contemporaries" including some selected works from Ceylonese, I am happy to be able to respond, in some measure, to the invitation of the Japanese Cultural Forum—organizers of this Exhibition—to provide this note attempting a glimpse into the ancient art of Ceylon and contemporary work, with particular emphasis on painting.

The history of the Fine Arts of Ceylon is as old as the history of the Island itself. It begins about the 5th century B.C., with the Colonization of the Island by an Aryan-speaking people from North India—the ancestors of the Sinhalese of today.

The introduction of Buddhism, in the middle of the 3rd century by Mahinda, the son of the Great Indian Emperor Asoka, during the reign of Devanampiyatissa (247–207 B.C.) witnessed the most important event in Sinhalese Culture.

Another early Sinhalese King, Duttagamini, described as the Asoka of Ceylon, for his zeal in the propagation of Buddhism, must be mentioned. The art of Ceylon, like the Gothic art of Europe, was never divorced from religion. For a correct assessment of the early period one turns to Dr. S. Paranavitana, until recently Archaeological Commissioner and now Professor of Archaeology in the University of Ceylon:

" The elements of culture which the early settlers brought with them enriched by Mauryan contacts and stimulated by the spiritual impulses of the Buddhist faith, developed in course of time to that aspect of the Great Indian civilization which is distinctive of Ceylon. New streams of culture continued to flow from the neighbouring Continent throughout the centuries, but the inherent conservative character of an Island people allowed but little modification, by these later Influences, by the Architectural forms and Artistic motifs which they had come to regard as their own. With the inevitable ups and downs, this civilization continued to be creative up to the 13th century, when signs of exhaustion set in."

In the study of Art in Ceylon, the historian is in a fortunate position in having for his reference the Great Chronicls of the Sinhalese, the Mahavansa, which gives a precise account of the reigns of her Kings and an accurate record of the methods ana building activities of the Kings throughout the 4th century. A later chronicles, the Culavamsa, carries the history into the 18th century.

Few cities in the history of this world remained capitals for 15 centuries; Rome the mighty lasted 1,000 years. But, Anuradhapura, first capital of Lanka, held its place of honour for a millenium and a half. In the green-shadowed solitudes of Anuradhapura rise the ruins of this ancient city. Once completely engulfed by the jungle waves, they have been reclaimed so that some idea of the grandeur of the capital is now afforded to any visitor. Charged with history, the monuments of Anuradhapura have stored up the energy of the past to release it to the present and to the future. Ruvanveli, Jetavana, Abhayagiri—colossal Dagobas; Thuparama, the dainty and Lanka-rama, with chisselled monoliths ringing them around; Sapling of Wisdom Tree, Bo, pulsating with life for 23 centuries; austere lithic porch and slab of Western monasteries, home of an ascetic school; park which gave peace to recluse; huge reservoirs (tanks) giving life, giving beauty and health; pleasance and bath house; sculptured moonstone; grace of guard stone; the form reverently set in poetic stone of the Teacher in whose ways walked a people for generation upon generation; O of these was the essence of A'pura, capital without peer.

Continual raids by the Tamils of South India forced the abandonment of Anuradhapura in the eighth century. From 781 to 1290 the Capital was Polonnaruwa, where the greatest period of artistic activity coincides with the reign of Parakrama Bahu the Great (1164–79).

THE GREAT STUPAS.

Dominating the landscape at Anuradhapura and Polonnaruwa are the most impressive monuments, the Great Stupas or Dagobas. They are the earliest forms of building now found in Ceylon. The Dagobas are classified by the shape of the dome; bell-shaped, bubble-shaped or lotus-shaped; and sometimes in the shape of a heap of paddy. The first Stupa, according to the Mahavamsa, is the Thuparama in A'pura (circa 307–267 B.C.). It originally had the shape of a paddy heap. The largest Stupa in Anuradhapura, the Jetawana (4th century A.D.) is said to have been 400 ft. in height originally and even as it is today stands at 281 ft. One of the largest of all the Stupas is the Ruwanweli Dagoba at Anuradhapura built by Dutta Gamini, the recent renovation of which alone took some 75 years. Benjamin Rowland says: "This monument is roughly one and a half times the size of the Great Stupa at Amaravati: the diameter of the dome is 204 feet and the height of the pinnacle more than 180 ft. above ground. The dimensions of this and other dagobas at Anuradhapura are as great as all but the largest of the Egyptian pyramids." Conforming to one pattern, these stupas consisted of a basal terrace of three stages. The dome was surmounted by a solid cube of brick masonry which was a series of umbrellas. The frontispieces or altars (Vahalkadas) at the cardinal points of these Stupas were excellent examples of architectural skill; the limestone stelae which flanked them contain some of the oldest specimens of plastic art of Ceylon, e.g., Kantaka Cetiya, Mihintale. Bas-relief of these frontispieces have close affinity to the bas-reliefs of Bharut and Sanchi.

Next to the Stupa, in historical and aesthetic importance is the Vatadage —the round relic house, which serves to cover the Stupa; it consists of rows of pillars of stone and a domical roof of wood, one of the best preserved examples of which is at Madirigiriya.

SCULPTURE

The school of sculptural art in Ceylon in early times came into contact with the more mature art of Andhra in India, and according to Dr. Paranavitana, the earliest type of the Buddha image in the round, with right shoulder bare, and the drapery shown in regular schematic folds in relief. The well-known Buddha, seated in attitude of meditation (all Buddhist images found in Ceylon with the exception of one are in the attitude of meditation) near the Abhayagiri Dagoba at Anuradhapura, is an exquisite work of about the 4th century. It is said that this image has affinities to the type of Buddha found in the later cave temples of Ajanta.

Dr. Paranavitana says: "The artists of old Ceylon had achieved no small measure of success in what they, in common with the artists of other Buddhist lands, aimed at in fashioning an image of the Master—to visualize the Great Sage as the embodiment of Supreme Wisdom and unbounded Compassion, serene in the peace of Nirvana. These two ideals of Wisdom and Compassion correspond to strength and grace in the aesthetic sphere and it is very rarely that perfect harmony of the two has been achieved in plastic form. The masterpieces of the Gupta age in India generally emphasized the quality of grace—this is in keeping with the emphasis which the Mahayanists laid on Karuna, Compassion. The best Buddha images of Ceylon, on the other hand, bring to the fore the quality of strength. The ancient Sinhalese artists evidently contemplated on the Buddha more as Dasabala than as Mahakarunika."

The colossus at Aukana, carved almost in the round and measuring 42 feet in height (with the pedestal), has been described by many as one of the finest stone statues of the Buddha in all Asia; of the well-known group of images at the Gal Vihara, the most impressive are a colossal rock-cut Parinirvana image nearly 50 feet in length and the standing figure of Ananda, nearly

25 feet high. Of similar grace and magnitude is the colossal figure of the Great King Parakkrama Bahu at Potgul Vehera, overlooking the waters of Topawewa at Polonnaruwa, which has been described as one of the finest pieces of Sculpture in Ceylon, "in spite of its great scale and weight, it has something of the feeling of the bronzes of the Chola Period—the suggestion of a moment of suspended animation, and the communication of the idea that the figure may at any moment stir into action."

The cultural relationship between India and Ceylon is revealed by the two well-known pieces of sculpture. One of them at Isurumuni in Anuradhapura is a bas-relief of a pair of Lovers on a granite slab, which is remarkable for its unity of composition and balance, reminiscent of Gupta art; while in pure Pallava style, close to the work at Mamallapuram in India, is the representation of the sculpture of Man and Horse. This is generally accepted as one of the masterpieces of the plastic art in Ceylon. Lawrence Binyon has referred to this sculpture as a 'tremendous work, impossible to forget when once seen.' This work aroused the curiosity of men of the stature of Dr. Coomaraswamy, Dr. Vincent Smith, Prof. Vogel and Dr. William Cohen. Dr. Paranavitana, in a valuable article in 'Artibus Asiae' argues the identity of this sculpture.

In the earliest phase, the architecture of the Sinhalese was essentially wooden; but little or nothing remains of the early structures recorded in the chronicles. The only master-pieces of wooden architecture which exist today are two magnificient pillared-halls—the Audience Hall in Kandy and the Digge (Drumming Hall) at the Embekke Devale—of the Kandyan and Gampola Periods respectively. They are notable for the remarkable wood carvings. Of the famous Audience Hall in Kandy, with its ornate pillars and characteristic high-pitched roof, much has been written and many a visitor to Kandy has seen it; but few perhaps, until recently, have seen the masterpieces at Embekke, Gampola. Embekke which must have been the inspiration for the work at the Audience Hall in Kandy provides the finest examples of Sinhalese craftsmanship in wood, the work of men who belonged to the College of Wood Sculpture of old. Local craftsmen, claiming lineal succession from the original masters, have played their part in the restoration of this work recently by the Archaeological Department.

The use of stone for the flights of steps, doorways and pillars was a common feature in ancient architecture, and these often received sculptural embellishments, e.g., steps carrying lotus-petal mouldings and figures of dwarfs (door-keepers) and the side balustrades ornamented with stylized figures of the Makara. Two exquisite examples of architectural embellishments in stone are the Guard-stones and "Moon-stones". The decorative scheme of the moonstone (a semi-circular slab of stone at the flight of steps in the shape of a half-moon) consists of an ornamental border, a row of animals (elephant, horse, lion and bull shown as if in movement chasing one another) a floral pattern, a row of geese and a frieze of lotus petals. The best three examples of the moon-stone found in Anuradhapura are considered to be masterpieces of Oriental Art.

BRONZES

Ceylon can count on a number of works of art produced in metal, mostly bronze, from the very early periods of Buddhist art. The best known of these is a graceful female statue of brass—the figure is obviously that of a goddess, popularly identified as Pattini. It is now in the British Museum. The great beauty of modelling of the torso and the clinging drapery is reminiscent of Gupta Workmanship; but according to Benjamin Rowland, the closest stylistic comparison for this figure is in the apsaras of the Sigiriya frescoes with the same exaggerated fullness of the breasts and narrow waist combined with an elaborate towering head-dress as in the Sigiriya " Nymphs ". The image is assigned to the 8th century and is said to have come from North Eastern Ceylon. The various Hindu temples or Siva Devales, (shrines erected during the Chola occupation in the 11th century) uncovered in the jungles of Polonnaruwa have brought to light some of the finest bronzes of the Hindu renaissance said to be earlier than any specimens known in India. Among these is the magnificent statue of Nataraja (now in the Colombo Museum) and the statue of Sundaramurthyswamy. These obviously came from South India or are the works of artists who hailed from that country. Numerous examples of Buddha Images in bronze have been found—at Ruvanveli Dagoba and the Mandala Giri Vihare. Quite recently, four figures of bronze horsemen which are unlike any other object of antique art found in India or Ceylon have been brought to light in the course of restoration work at the ancient Stupa at Mahiyangana (11th century). They have been identified as representatives of Asvins, the Indian Deities, who had an important place in Vedic Religion.

The Sinhalese were also reputed for exquisite work in Ivory, Gold and Silver, and recent excavations revealed a high quality of pottery as well.

LONG PICTORIAL TRADITION

Ceylon had had a long pictorial tradition; Tennent, an eminent historian, once claimed for Ceylon the origin of oil painting; but when one talks of the Fine Arts of Ceylon, our minds naturally go back to the oldest and best preserved fresco paintings of the 5th century found in a cavity of the rock at Sigiriya, the ancient rock-fortress of parricide King Kassapa. They depict profusely bejewelled females, like Apsaras rising from the clouds, cut off at the waist. Some of them are of a fragmentary character. Of the hundreds of such figures which once adorned this Rock Gallery, only 21 remain; it must indeed have been a unique aesthetic experience and visitors of the eighth and ninth centuries had been inspired into song and some hundreds of verses embodying their reactions have been scrawled on the glossy walls of the Gallery. Thanks to Dr. S. Paranavitana, these graffiti have been deciphered and compiled. And we learn, inter alia, that art criticism too was not unknown among the ancient Sinhalese. Of the aesthetic value of these paintings, Benjamin Rowland says:

> "In studying these works we are struck at once by the robust strength of both the drawing and colouring. That the draughtsmanship was entirely free hand becomes apparent when we note the many corrections, changes not only in the colours but complete alterations

of the positions of the hands of certain figures. The swelling, nubile breasts, the tiny waist—hardly greater than the girth of the neck— the shapely tapered arms and exquisitely poised flower-like hands— these are all elements of the same canon that determined the types of physical beauty in the wall paintings of India proper. Here these charms are rendered even more provocative through their exaggeration. The resemblance of these figures to the maidens of the Amaravati reliefs suggests their derivation from a lost school of Andhra painting. If the boldness of the drawing and the brilliance of the colours are recognizable as typically Sinhalese, the actual physical types represented, with heavy-lidded eyes, sharp aquiline noses, and full lips, may be taken as direct reflexions of actual Sinhalese types.

A rather distinctive technical feature of the Sigiriya paintings is the method of drawing the noses. Of these are two distinct types: in one of these conceptual preservations the nose is represented in profile, although the face may be in three-quarter view; the second method shows the nose in three-quarter view, with the further nostril clearly defined. Another interesting technical aspect is the manner in which the individual brush-strokes, as in the painting of the breasts, make a surface pattern and at the same time reinforce the form."

Dr. Ananda Coomaraswamy (Mediaeval Sinhalese Art) says: "The work is much freer and shows greater knowledge of the human figure than any work now done; perhaps, we cannot judge much from this single surviving example of what must have been a Great School, working over a very extended area. Their one great value is the demonstration of the fact that the work of the Ajanta School was so widespread."

Indeed, Ajanta is dear not only to India but also to the whole world. The influence of Ajanta is evident in the art of the whole of Asia. We see derivations of the Ajanta idiom in the frescoes of Horyu-ji in Japan, Tung Hwang in China, Bamiyang in Afghanistan, the banner paintings of Tibet and Nepal, and Sigiriya in Ceyon. Ajanta is thus the fountain-head of a world tradition, so to speak. Somebody said that since the last painter laid down his brush at Sigiriya till we come to the Kandyan period there was a hiatus in the history of painting in Ceylon. This is not the case. Fragmentary paintings at Hindagala, near Kandy, reveal the work of a school closely allied with the later phase of the art of Ajanta. Likewise, the fragment of a painting found in a cave near Dimbulagala in the North Central Province, is assigned to the same period; of the 12th to the 13th century paintings, there remain some fine examples on the walls of the Tivanka Shrine (popularly known as the Northern Temple) at Polonnaruwa where a series of frescoes depict the life of the Buddha and the Jataka stories. According to Dr. Paranavitana, these indicate that "the classic Buddhist art retained its vitality in Ceylon up to a comparatively late period. These paintings no doubt show a deterioration in quality when compared with the masterpieces of more spacious days, but even in the 12th century the Sinhalese painter was capable of expressive and delicate work, could give plasticity to his figures, and understood the principles of balanced composition."

A couple of years ago, opening the relic chamber at Mahiyangana Stupa, one of the holiest shrines of Ceylon Buddhism, archaeologists had an unexpected surprise—ancient paintings. It was earlier known from the chronicles that in ancient Ceylon the walls of relic chambers were at times decorated with paintings, but hitherto a chamber so adorned had not been brought to light. From the fragments of painting discovered it has been possible to reconstruct a number of figures which are an important addition to the specimens of ancient paintings which this country can boast of. The largest fragment depicts the seated Buddha under the Bodhi tree and the main scene appears to have been the Enlightenment of the Buddha, on which occasion the Gods and Brahmas were said to have come to pay homage to the Great Sage. Rated very high on aesthetic grounds, these paintings reveal a sure line with delicate shading. They have been ascribed on stylistic ground to a date earlier than the 11th century. But Dr. Paranavitana adds: "It is, of course, possible to argue that artistic styles remained relatively constant in Ceylon, and that a work produced here in the 11th century could bear the same characteristics as a painting from India belonging to the 7th or 8th centuries."

Centuries after the fall of Polonnaruwa in 1213, the jungle enveloped the ancient cities where art flourished; new cities rose in other parts of the Island, but not of the same grandeur and scale as before. The decorative element in art continued but the heroic scale of work disappeared.

Mediaeval fresco painting as a whole has not received the study and attention it deserves; the popular notion that all wall painting after Sigiriya is decadent has no doubt been largely responsible for this attitude. It is as fallacious to say that after Sigiriya nothing noteworthy exists in the realm of painting. Perhaps, it would be closer to the truth to say that there is no Sinhalese Sculpture of note after Avukana or Gal Vihare. Dr. Ananda Coomaraswamy's monumental work—Mediaeval Sinhalese Art alone remains the only pioneer study of peasant art and the way of life of the Sinhalese Craftsmen in Ceylon: Widely acknowledged as one of the greatest art critics and philosophers of art of the twentieth century, Dr. Coomaraswamy says: "Owing in a large measure to the activities of King Kirthi Sri Raja Sinha, who was such an eager friend of religion and art, we find preserved a sufficient amount of 18th century painting. The few really good painters of this traditional line, now living, are equal to any but the very best 18th century men, such as Devaragampola Silvatenna Unnanse, who painted Jatakas at Ridi Vihare and at Degaldoruwa". That was in 1908. Mr. D. B. Dhanapala, in his story of Sinhalese painting just published, compiles a useful record of the more important frescoes of Ceylon. The 18th century work may be best studied in old and unrestored Viharas, such as Degaldoruwa and Ridi Vihare.

At a recent conference on traditional Cultures in Ceylon, initiated by UNESCO, a case for the revival of Kandyan Painting was re-opened by Dr. Gunesinghe of the University of Ceylon: He said: "Reviving is probably the wrong word if it gives anybody the idea that the attempt is to bring to life something that is altogether dead: Kandyan Painting is not dead. If it is dead, it is so only in the eyes of those who are not aware of its existence. It is no more dead today than Kandyan Dancing (*Pl. 12*) was two decades ago. It only awaits to be recognized. And that is just what we mean by reviving: to recognize Kandyan temple painting as a particular style of painting that deserves to be practised and appreciated. This depends of course on how satisfying aesthetically Kandyan painting is, and this kind of judgment depends entirely on what sort of art education we have."

Coomaraswamy observes:—"In Kandyan painting there is an entire absence of perspective and shading. The primary object is to tell an edifying story in an attractive way. The work is thus rather epic in character than artistic in the modern sense. It has a great deal in common with the mural painting of Egypt; in its pure gay colour, decorative flat treatment and restfulness, it is most admirable as wall painting...... The most essential character of Kandyan painting, as of Kandyan design in general, is its idealism. This idealism belongs to all Indian art; but in Kandyan art it appears in almost an extreme form...... Kandyan art does not represent Indian art at its greatest or even at a very great period, but rather Indian art at the level of a great and beautiful scheme of peasant decoration. Kandyan art represents a tradition handed down from the earliest stratum of Indian Art, modified and enriched by subsequent influences."

Sinhalese Arts and Crafts flourished under the system of service tenures which prevailed in those early days; every craftsman enjoyed his assignment of lands and paddy fields in return for his services to the State and Society. It was a system particularly conducive to the growth of arts and crafts. The craftsmen were, however, not by any means serfs, nor adscriptus glebae, because a tenant always had the right to refuse service and surrender his lands. He held an honourable place in Society. Old records mention names of kings as having been craftsmen. For example, Jettatissa (A.D. 332) was a skilful carver. "This monarch, having carried out several arduous undertakings in painting and carving, himself taught the art to many of his subjects. He sculptured a beautiful image of the Bodhistatva, so perfect that it seemed as if it had been executed by supernatural power; and also a throne, a parasol and a State Room with some beautiful works in ivory made for it."

The two chief factors that contributed to the high development of the Arts in Ceylon was a patronage and economic security. As Dr. G. P. Malalaskera, erstwhile Dean of the Faculty of Oriental Studies of the University of Ceylon, presently Ceylon's first Ambassador to Moscow, once put it: "Our artistic vitality never died; it was only lowered by circumstances beyond our control."

What was once a vital movement has become enfeebled and degenerated into merely pretty or decorative futilities; insipid copies of Sigiriya and meaningless compositions described as "Oriental" art have become the order of the day; but the school of traditional painting still lives with the Sittaras, despite the worst type of representational Western techniques now found in modern temples.

In modern temple painting, the only works of any significance in recent times are to be found on the walls of the famed Kelaniya Temple near Colombo the work of Solius Mendis; in the heart of Colombo, at Gotami Vihare, Borella, George Keyt (*Pl. 10*) has produced an Indian raga ("mode") in paint: both these are on a heroic scale—the former retaining the traditional manner and the latter a happy merger of Ajanta plus Picasso. Another noteworthy mural of modern times is the work of David Paynter, Principal of the Government College of Fine Arts, done at the Trinity College Chapel in Kandy.

In low-country Ceylon, the best examples of traditional mural paintings are to be found at Kelaniya, Sailabimbaramaya, Mulgirigala and Telwatta.

THE CONTEMPORARY SCENE

To come to the contemporary scene more intimately, painting in Ceylon falls into three categories; the 'oriental', the academic and the modern; the 'Orientalists' have made their revivalist painting a call back to old patterns. They have produced little of any significance so far. The sugariness and superficial finish of these imitations of Sigiriya or the erstwhile Bengal School reveal that they are going through a period which India has just left; it is best to remind that there is a danger in the prolongation of the revivalist mood after its historical necessity is over. This feeling disappeared in India when the radical movement in Indian painting was founded by the Tagores, Amrita Sher Gil and Jamini Roy. And today, Indian artists accept suggestions from all over the world and the best of them assimilate these and create new significances of their own and the variety and vitality of contemporary urges predominate. Trying to reproduce the best of the past cannot perpetuate itself for all time without stifling creative imagination.

The Victorian tradition of the Ceylonese painter of today is born of the English education which most of the middle and upper classes have received for nearly two centuries. Among them are a number of estimable and accomplished painters who have won renown both in Ceylon and Britain; but the vast majority of them go for the picturesque (sunsets, flamboyants, yellow robes) and "head-hunting"—portraiture—and their works are apt to be flatly uninspired; but there is among them a greater degree of honesty in Art, a belief in the fundamentals of good drawing and draftsmanship as compared to the camp-followers of the genuine 'modernist': To put it in the words of a contemporary Ceylon painter, "the present craze in Ceylon for "non-representational" or "abstract" art, which is the most reactionary and least logical (and fortunately for the untalented, the easiest) of all forms of revolutionary painting, still has a dwindling following abroad and a vast one here. Fashions are frequently discarded elsewhere before they reach us."

Then there are those who began to turn their attention to the principles of simplification and significant form which had guided Neo-Impressionist and post Impressionist art in Europe—the art of Cezanne, Van Gogh and Gauguin—many of these principles which are to be found in Classical Sinhalese or Indian Sculpture. Sections of the Ceylon public nevertheless are ever ready to deride modern European art that it thus betrays ignorance of guiding principles of the ancient art of the East; modern European art is, I believe, the off-shoot of a great oriental tree: And it was Eric Newton who said: "Behind every Western carving of the human figure is the implication of a portrait; behind every oriental statue is the implication of a mood. The idea of serenity has never been quite so intensely caught and held by any European sculptor as it has by countless of the cross-legged

Buddhas of Ceylon." The prejudice against modern European art is unfortunately too often occasioned by work which masquerades under that name.

The best tribute to Ceylon's modern group, the '43 Group (so called since its inauguration in 1943), has been paid by William Graham, writing in the STUDIO (London), whose introductory words supply the key to contemporary painting: Graham says: "The most significant movement in Eastern art today is to be found in Ceylon. Its importance lies in the synthesis of traditional art forms and those deriving from the West, which has produced painting truly Eastern in inspiration, yet of universal validity. Its great vitality springs from a contemplative humanist vision, which gives an imagination and lyrical interpretation of the life of the Island; it is an art at once profound and optimistic.

The factors governing the growth of modern painting in Ceylon lies in the happy circumstances of her recent history. Her peaceful progress to political independence, free from the strife and bitterness which retarded artistic growth elsewhere in the East, allowed the artist, while rediscovering his native heritage, to continue to assimilate the best Western influences. This essential union of regard for the past and awareness of the present was wholly favourable to creative activity. Western influence, however, had not always been beneficial. During nearly four centuries of Portuguese, Dutch and British occupation, Ceylonese culture was in eclipse, and the old aristocracy was replaced by a rich urban class whose social and cultural standards were those of the West. Colonial education introduced alien standards of art until, in the 19th century, the worst kind of Victorian naturalism became the goal of artistic accomplishment.

With the decline of Western power, and the consequent rapid growth of Ceylonese nationalism at the beginning of this century, came a re-awakened pride in native culture which rapidly gained in prestige following the first World War. A new intelligentsia emerged, and the study of ancient Oriental art was stimulated. This re-discovery ranged over the vast field of sculpture and painting existing in the buried cities of the Island, the art of A'pura, of Polonnaruwa, of Sigiriya and the Jataka fable painting of the Kandyan period, in addition to the mural paintings in villages and temples. This great heritage was characterized by a contemplative view of the peaceful and ordinary aspects of life, and had an immediate appeal and stimulus for the aesthetic temperament of modern Ceylonese artists, indicating to them not so much how they should create as how they should look at the life around them. These artists were no less aware of the present and of the growing internationalism of all art, and they realized that exterior forces must be reckoned with if their art was to find its right context in the pattern of world culture. A few of them studied in Europe where they were much impressed by the closeness with which aesthetic feeling of modern European painting approached that of ancient Ceylon, while the reproductions which they brought back greatly influenced other painters."

The contemporary painters who have contributed much towards the development of painting, and who have been the biggest influences are Justin Daraniyagala, George Keyt (*Pl. 10*), Harry Pieris of the '43 Group; Geoffrey Beling, Chief Inspector of Art who has been largely responsible for accelerating modern methods of art education in Ceylon schools; Aubrey Collette, the brilliant Cartoonist and painter, the greatest single influence in Ceylon journalism since the late Mr. D.R. Wijewardene. A.C.G.S. Amarasekera, J.D.A. Perera, David Paynter and Stanley Abeyesinghe of the Ceylon Society of Arts; Manjusri, Sakalasuriya Sowabandu, and Ananda Samarakoon, the main forces of the 'Oriental' school. The work of those mentioned forms the solid foundation of today's achievement. Following them are many young painters of great promise, a few of whom are represented at this show (*Pls. 11 and 12*). Their's will be the responsibility of the future.

Samuel Butler wrote that the history of art is the hisory of revivals. The art of Ceylon never died and not all of Ceylonese art has slumbered; As Coomaraswamy put it "there are still sufficient traces of the old national life, sufficient remains of skilful craftsmen's handiwork." Independence saw Ceylon on the threshold of a renaissance of her traditional arts; it opened the door to the growth of a creative activity, particularly in the field of handicrafts: the Festivals of the Arts organized by the Ceylon Society of Arts, the work of the Rural Development and Cottage Industries Department, the Lanka Mahila Samitis (Women's Institutes), the Kalutara Basket Society, the Kandyan Art Association, the Sinhala Institute of Culture and the Government College of Fine Arts contributed much towards the revival and improvement of local handicrafts—a heritage which any country could be proud of. The establishment of the Arts Council of Ceylon, largely due to the enlightened vision of Ceylon's first Governor-General, Lord Soulbury, was warmly welcomed by all who have at heart the restoration of the arts and craftsmanship and culture for which Ceylon was famous many centuries ago. The Council has done much to assist and stimulate the many activities—and Ceylonese art which encountered the fate of the Sleeping Beauty in the old French fairy tale has awakened, to a life of vigour, vitality and usefulness. How much of these traditional treasures of handicrafts can survive the challenge of modernity? The answer, as usual, depends on the capacity of its inheritors to adopt the traditional designing to the changing needs and attitudes of the modern man without destroying its essential spirit. The need for change is imperative. It is clear that design development has to be informed by a clear sense of direction. It would not be out of place to say that it would be well to obtain the technical 'know-how' and modern methods of handicraft designing, the improvement of tools and processes from Japan, (Japan has already assisted the Ceylon Cottage Industries Department with experts in handicrafts under the Colombo Plan Technical Cooperation Scheme.) with a view to better marketability and aesthetic values. The problems of technical improvement are many.

Some recent efforts to revive Kandyan Dancing, one of the traditional arts, should not go unrecorded. Kandyan dancing refers to those typical forms of traditional dance that has survived only in the Kanda Uda Rata or Central Hills of Ceylon. Mr. Arthur Molamure, a well-known local authority points out that its affinities with Indian forms are unmistakable probably indicative of a common source; the evident dissimilarities are such that Kandyan Dancing may be regarded as a distinct species possessing in its own right the attributes of refinement and distinction associated with such highly evolved Indian forms as Kathakali or Bharata-Natyam. Its technique is stylized, developed far beyond the stage of merely "folk" and exemplifies an aristocratic and classical tradition inherited from the past although its exponents are peasant cultivators, not solely dependent for their livelihood on the profession of dancing. Beryl de Zoete, well-known authority on the dances of the East, gives the contemporary situation: "It has become the custom of late years to send young dancers from Ceylon to study dancing in India. Nothing could be better (except studying their own dances) if they really studied thoroughly one of the classical schools of Indian Dance. But they generally return with a curious hybrid called "Oriental Dancing" composed of a smattering of all schools—Kathak, Manipuri, Kathkali and Bharatanatyam—and if they have got so far as Santiniketan, a Santal folk dance or two thrown in. This confusion of styles does not enrich Ceylon, which has already some of the finest dances in the world." But in fairness it must be said that some leading choreographers and dancers have evolved fascinating Ballet, born of this Indian experience. They include dancers like Chitra Sena, Premkumar, Pani Bharata and Vasanta Kumar—all of whom were well received recently in Moscow.

The revivalist movement has also seen the development of Low Country dancing, folk dance-drama and Sinhalese drama.

Mention must be made of the presentation of Maname—the Sinhalese folk drama, in operatic style by the University players under the guidance of Dr. E.R. Sarathchandra and Charles Silva Gurunance; and the production of the best Sinhalese film so far—Rekava, under the direction of Lester James Peiris. These were notable art events of recent times.

With the Sinhalese language given its rightful place and the creation of a separate Ministry of Cultural Affairs, there is a hope for the future in the development of the creative arts of the country. Much is expected of the young University of Ceylon—past, present and future, and we look to them to carry on the great cultural work. There are eminent Orientalists, the first Ceylonese Commissioner of Archaeology of whom any country might well be proud. Much remains to be done in revealing what the jungle and the soil still hide of the two great cities of the past, and much research on what has already been brought to light. The ancient city of Anuradhapura is now safely preserved—the hideous modern township that grew upon the site of the old city is being removed and a new town of Anuradhapura established—preserving the spirit, atmosphere and grandeur of the old "for the serene joy and emotion of the pious"—and the scholar: incidentally, the first step in the implementation of this preservation scheme was taken by the Hon. Mr. S.W.R.D. Bandaranaike, the present Prime Minister, when he was Minister of Local Government.

I could do no better than recall Benjamin Rowland:

> "Ceylon provides a setting particularly congenial to the study of Buddhist art, not only because of its great beauty and the amiability of its people, but also because there, in the great veneration accorded the ancient monuments by the people—sometimes carried to unfortunate extremes of renovation—the student feels that the subject is much more part of a living tradition."

IMPORTANCE OF CULTURAL EXCHANGES.

It has been rightly pointed out on occasions that in the sphere of art, as in other spheres, Ceylon should guard against extreme isolationism. The fact that different artistic traditions cannot be ultimately assimilated does not justify the hermetic sealing of a nation's art. Almost every nation has borrowed something from another and Ceylon can borrow from the East and the West without danger or detriment to her own individuality.

Recent exhibitions sponsored by the Society of Arts, the Arts Council and the National Commission of UNESCO and other organizations locally include exhibitions of the work of India, Pakistan, Burma, Indonesia, Japan, China, Canada, United States of America and the United Kingdom—these have done much to accelerate the exchange of cultural relationships and aesthetic standards. I would like to refer particularly to the exhibition of Japanese wood colour prints sponsored by the National Committee of Plastic Artists of Ceylon and the Deparment of National Museums, Ceylon, assisted by the Ministry of Cultural Affairs and the Japanese Embassy in Colombo. The exhibits which included reproductions of early Ukiyoe prints, modern woodcut prints and works of contemporary artists of the Ukiyoe school (which included the work of Shiko Munakata who won the international prize at the Venice Biennale of 1956 and came first in South America's great art show) proved a stimulating and rich experience to the local artists.

CHINESE PAINTING

Chinese painting stands alone in the realm of art and holds a unique position between the East and the West. From the nineteenth century, it won much wider appreciation, and today it is almost a mainstay of art in the world.

In thought, Chinese painting follows the course ascribed to three traditional philosophies: Confucianism, Taoism and Chan, or Zen Buddhism.

In technique, Chinese painting is evaluated by brush-work done flatly.

In spirit, Chinese painting emancipates such lyricism as is derived from fine strokes, anatomical structure, and rhythmic composition.

In short, Chinese painting is the combined product of five elements: profundity of learning, meditation, nobility of character, talent, and painstaking effort. Below is a brief history of its origin and development.

Chinese painting evolved from picture-writing, which began with symbols transcribing ideas structural as well as abstract. For instance, a natural object like water at first took the form of ∫ as a symbol; later a double ∫∫ expressed its movement; and still later the multiple ∭ indicated a flowing current. Again, an object like the sun was at first drawn as ○; later as ◎; and still later as ◎ ◎ ◎ ◎ ◎ to express a more complicated view. When evolved into writing, such pictograms, geometrical as they are, underwent slight changes so that water took the form ∬, while the sun became ⊙. Thus, pictogram and pictography developed side by side.

Complicated symbolic words identify themselves with symbolic pictures. For instance, the 暴 is said to indicate an aspect of agricultural life. According to *Su Wen*, a book on the origin of Chinese writing, this character, alternately written as 晞, takes its origin from the forms of sunrise, straw and rice, and as such clearly indicates the idea of taking out straw and rice for drying at sunrise. Another interesting example is the word 光, written in spiral-script as 光. So Wen interprets it as brightness shed from the light on a desk; while Chin Wen, a still older spiral-script, writes it as 光, which clearly describes a man kneeling before a fire. Thus we know that there was fire-worship among our earliest ancestors, and the picture has been inseparable from writing ever since.

In Neolithic earthwares excavated in the provinces of Honan and Kansu, pictorial decoration was found on a few pieces of pottery. In later Neolithic painted pottery unearthed at Liang Shao, Ma Chang, and Hsin Tien, there have been pieces even bearing geometrical forms in reddish brown and grey, with one clay cover showing the profile of a human-figure, so cleverly done that it succeeds in conveying the mood of the man at play. Aesthetics had already dawned in the mind of men.

This fact was further borne out by the inscribed bones unearthed at Yin Su. Although the pictograms were incised with some kind of pointed instrument, they already showed a high aesthetic sense in form delineation, design, and style.

When the pictogram evolved to this stage, human thought attained maturity, and artistic aspiration went along with it.

Bronze-ware unearthed from the shores of the Yellow River also had a variety of pictograms which were apparently decorations for ceremonial utensils. These works clearly indicate an advanced stage of aesthetic development.

Among the latest finds at Changsha from a Chou Dynasty tomb is a silk painting which looks entirely different from those inscribed on stone, pottery and bronze. At the upper right is painted a phoenix signifying life and peace; at the upper left, one-legged animal indicating disaster and death; and underneath them is the image of a girl praying, evidently radiant for her victory in the struggle.

Most primitive pictograms, except those with symbolic purposes, were utilitarian. Thus the Emperor Huang Ti, painted garments in a campaign against the rebel Chi Yu; King Yu and King Shun kept clothes and hats so decorated as to distinguish official ranks. Paintings appeared in different forms on ceremonial utensils, such as banners, vestments, cooking or drinking vessels, weapons and the like. All these, besides being art, served the purpose either of admonition or cultural promotion, and all are as realistic as Confucianism could make them.

During the period of Ch'un Ch'iu and the Warring States, Chinese painting took a new turn. A story is told of a painter in the State of Ch'i who had left his wife at home for years and was often lonely for her, and who ran through his imagination and painted her portrait. This has nothing to do with ethical or religious motives, but rather exemplifies the growth of individual inspirations, thus paving the way for emotional paintings in later generations.

These first beginnings in pictorial expression met a hard fate at the hands of Shih Huang Ti of the Ch'in Dynasty. What remains worthy of mention from his reign is the story of an artist who used his toes to paint a figure and another man, a labourer in the Court of Shih Huang, who depicted the God of the Sea, also with his foot. This bespeaks a decline in Chinese art.

When the Han epoch came, in the wake of considerable chaos, Taoism and painting were both in vogue. The emperors Wen and Ching used the visual arts in politics, and King Wu in particular engaged many artists, assembled all the valuable calligraphic works and paintings that could be ransacked throughout the kingdom and gathered around him many virtuoso officers for the study and appreciation of art. Thus for the first time art stepped into imperial court. From the reign of Emperor Kuang Wu up to that of Emperor Ming, Chinese painting was imbued with the smell of Confucianism. This marks the start of religious painting, a momentous fact in the chronicle of Chinese art.

It was during the reign of Emperor Ming that Buddhism was imported into China from India. Many a Buddhist temple was erected, and the White Horse Temple was embellished with mural paintings which came as a shock to the artistic world. This is the first stage in incorporating Buddhist painting into Chinese art.

The most revered artists of this period are Mao Yen-shou, Chang Hêng, Ts'ai Yung, Chao Ch'i, and Liu Yü. Mao Yen-shou was a craftsman; Chang Hêng was well versed in classics; and both Chao Ch'i and Liu Yü were high officers. We can thus see that Han painters were invariably men of parts, and this explains the special characteristic of Chinese artists in distinction to those of other counties.

In period of Wei and Tsing, the conservatism of Confucianism in Han painting could no longer be maintained, and Taoism soon stepped in to take its place. This, coupled with the vogue of meditation and the products of leading literati, immediately changed the outlook on life and on painting as well. Paintings of Buddhas were exalted as they had not been earlier. While previous works had used historic and classical stories as their themes, now most paintings were for churches or temples. Formerly, artists were mostly in the employment of the Court; now they could freely paint on their own.

When the Dynasty Tsing retreated to the South, the Northern areas were entirely occupied by barbarians. In the presence of beautiful Southern scenery such as they had never before seen, artists in exile saw fit to incorporate into their works ideal landscapes independent of figures and other details. With the emergence of landscape painting people began to regard a work of art as an object for appreciation rather than for utilitarian purposes, education, religion, decoration, propaganda, or whatever else. The position of art was thereby elevated and a rigid demarcation was drawn between artists and artisans, the former being devotees to fineness of brush-work and ink-tone, the latter being simply servicemen for a given purpose.

The earliest landscape painter, or perhaps the pioneer in the style, is Ku K'ai-chih to whom no surviving work can authentically be attributed but to whom were attributed voluminous articles on the technique of painting: e.g., an essay on how to convey the inner spirit, not through the eye alone, but through the mind aided by the eye. Such special treatises, together with a book on criticism of paintings, make him the most important art critic in the history of Chinese art. The famous Six Principles by Hsieh Ho was in fact but an outgrowth of Ku's writings. Ranking as high as Ku K'ai-Chih was Wang I, who gave us a book on the effect of intensive study; and Wang Hsi-Chih, son of Wang I, known as "the prince of calligraphers", who was a staunch advocate of individual personality. All these, allied with the Taoism of Lao-tzu and his disciple Chuang-tzu, constitute the very core of the Chinese conception of art, preciously treasured and diligently emulated by successors down to the present day.

When the Middle Kingdom was divided into the Northern and Southern Dynasties, the spread of Buddhism had a great impact on Chinese painting. The keenest exponents of the new religion were the Southern Liang and Northern Wei. Buddhism owed its growth chiefly due to encouragement by the emperors, particularly Emperor Tao Wu of the Northern Wei. Noted masters of this period are Ts'ao Fu-hsing, Lu T'an-wei, Ku K'ai-Chih and Chang Sêng-Yu, most of whom devoted their major effort to the portrayal of figures and scenes from the myths, legends, and history of the three religions, and most of whom mastered more than one technique.

In a sense, Taoism sprang from within China, and gained ground in and after the Later Han and Tsing. Thus, we may regard this as a period of mixture of the three great religions.

Painting of the Sui Dynasty shows no striking difference from that of the Tsing, although works adapted to Confucianism were emphasized.

The T'ang Dynasty is regarded by both Chinese and foreigner as the golden age of art and culture. The paintings of early Táng were mostly cultural; those of middle T'ang, literary; and works of late T'ang were signs at best of survival in a waning prosperity.

The most prominent artist of T'ang is Wu Tao-tzu, who has been called "the sage of painting" because of his versatility in every style and technique. Notwithstanding his talent, he was not a man of literary attainments; and doubt is moreover cast upon his character if the story is true that he hired a man to kill a famous contemporary painter.

Other contemporaries were Li Ssu-hsün, descendant of the first T'ang emperor, known as the Big General, and others to be discussed below. It is said that both Li Ssu-hsün and Wu Tao-tzu were once asked to paint on the palace walls Szechuan landscapes stretching well over 300 li. While Wu used bold strokes in his picture and completed it in a day, Li did his landscapes by very minute lines and staggeringly heavy colours in about a month. Yet both works were perfect. Li painted in a style of his own, and he has been known as the master of the "Northern School."

Close upon the heels of Wu and Li came the talented artist Wang Wei, who rose unrivalled as the father of the "Southern School" by introducing the landscape in monochrome. Such paintings are enlivened with the presence of nature. The brush-work and ink tone are so ideally blended as to ensure the effect of transcendence, solitude and mistiness evoked by the thought of Zen Buddhism. Small wonder that Wang's style at once won the highest esteem among scholars and officers. Wang Wei was also a man of high literary attainments; it has often been said that "his poems are like pictures, and his pictures, have the direct appeal of poetry."

It is to be noted that the "Northern School" and "Southern School" are distinguished not by different localities, but by a striking difference in styles. The former leans upon realism, heavily laid strokes or colours, while the latter stresses emotion as well as sensitive brush-work. Of the two, the "Southern School" has always been more highly esteemed.

Distinguished painters other than the three masters discussed above were Yen Li-pên, Yen Li-tê, Ts'ao Pa, Han Kan, Chou Fang, and Sun Wei. Another name of great prominence is the art critic Chang Yen-yüan, whose book on the appraisal of painting of the preceding dynasties is so thorough and profound that it has made the deepest impression on the minds of all Chinese artists. In brief, Chang held that "a painting should be evaluated beyond its verisimilitude"; that "the highest merit in a painting is its effect of lyricism"; that "calligraphic and pictorial strokes are inseparable"; and that "no common person can ever expect to render a work of fine art."

The Five Dynasties carried on the tradition passed down by T'ang of figures, landscapes, flowers, and birds. The masters of this period were Chin Hao, Kuang T'ung, and Tung Yüan. Kuang T'ung had been the pupil of Ching Hao, and was admired for his ability to enlarge the inherited technique. Of these three painters, Tung Yüan occupied the place of greatest importance, for he conveyed the mood of Southern scenery, in contrast to the bold style of Ching Hao and Kung T'ung.

The best flower-painters of this period were Hsü Hsi and Huang Ch'üan. Hsü Hsi with his grandson Hsü Ch'ung-Ssu were the pioneers in the technique of using no outline for the contour of an object. Huang Ch'üan and his son Huang Chü-ts'ai were pioneers in the technique of drawing contours with more than one layer of colour.

Like those of the Five Dynasties, paintings of the Sung era followed the trend from the T'ang period. T'ang was the turning point both in culture and art, and Sung harvested the mature product. Not only did Sung paintings tap literature as a source of development, but pictorial art was also interwoven with calligraphy. This period therefore gave us such great poet-artists as Su Tung-p'o, Wen Yü-k'o, Mi Fei, Li Kung-lin, Emperor Hui Tsung, and close followers such as Li Ch'êng, Fan K'uan, Chao Ling-Hsian, Chao Po-chü, Li T'ang, Liu Sung-nien, Ma Yüan, Hsia Kuei and Chü Jên. All of them were accomplished in literature. From this period non-literati could hardly gain a foothold in the realm of art, and it was felt that a scholar should be ashamed of being unable to understand painting, and a painter should be ashamed of ignorance in literature. This vogue has persisted to the present.

The Yüan Dynasty of the Mongol invaders at first produced nothing but military adventures. Before long, however, it adapted itself to Chinese culture and carried painting one step further. Confronted with the impressive scenery of the South, but denied any chance to express their grievances over the loss of territories, the Sung survivors gave vent to their feelings through ink, thus bringing the scholar's painting to the highest degree it had yet reached.

A scholar's painting does not depict life. Objects of concrete reality give place to imagination. Details, physical forms and even accuracy were thrown away in favour of the spirit or lyricism to be gained through fine brush-work and ink-gradation. This makes a contrast with the paintings of the Sung period, which attach importance to lively conveyance of physical, inner law, and with T'ang paintings, which simply stressed adherence to reality.

The earlier years of the Yüan Dynasty gave us such literati-painters as Chao Tzu-ang, Ch'ien Hsüan and Kao K'o-kung; and at its later stages came the four great Yüan masters: Huang Kung-wang, Ni Tsan, Wu Chên, and Wang Mêng.

The Yüan emphasis on spirit was enunciated by Huang Kung-wang when he stressed that "a painting is but an expression of one's conception"; that "the tone or atmosphere of a painting makes an indispensable criterion for evaluation;" and that "when both concept and atmosphere come into harmony, the highest skill in painting is fulfilled."

Apart from conception and tone, the effect of rhythm and stroke are equally important qualities to be stressed. Ni Tsan most distinguished for the quality of rhythm, said: "My bamboo paintings are intended merely to paint the fugitive spirit in my breast." In other words, the quality of rhythm is substantially an attempt to express an ideal derived from character and profound learning, while that of stroke demands the ability to incorporate into the brush-work one's inner emotion. Both aim at the expression of artistic genius, which it seems can only be expected from a qualified scholar.

The artists of the Ming Dynasty followed the footsteps of their predecessors; yet in many respects their works retained so much of the grandeur and gaiety of the T'ang period that they were almost a merger of all preceding techniques. Furthermore, a pedantic archaism also pervaded most Ming paintings, and shut off the possibility of innovation. This is generally considered a point of weakness. In evaluating the paintings of the four outstanding painters of this period, we readily see that Wên Chêng-ming managed to achieve serenity; Shên Ying, boldness; and T'ang-Yin, archaic grace. As for Ch'in Shih-chou, he was less accomplished in literature and he could do no better than Tung Ch'i-ch'ang, although we must grant his success in minute and delicate brush-work.

Imitation of earlier styles was the striking feature of Ch'ing painting. The influence of Western painting is not to be overlooked. These last two periods put too much emphasis on verisimilitude, a fact that explains why their works fail to arouse greater esteem. Nevertheless, the landscapes of Shih T'ao and the flower-and-bird paintings of Pa-ta Shan-jen, together with the flowers of Yün Nan-t'ien, were in artistic technique near Hsü Wei and Ch'en Pei-yang of the Ming Dynasty. No one can dispute the unusual dexterity of the four Wangs. Shih T'ao was not only a skillful painter, but also a first-rate art critic. He pointed out the necessity of building correct basic strokes as a prelude to more advanced attempts, for which insight he was acclaimed the best tutor for later learners. His essay, if clearly analyzed and interpreted, can stand comparison with the critical books of the world.

A terrible decline came during the Republican years. Many reasons might be cited: 1) a deterioration in the long artistic tradition, 2) the preponderance of Western thought, 3) the encroachment of foreign imperialism, 4) the unchecked power of party politics, 5) the spread of poverty, and 6) last but no less important, the popular feeling of unrest throughout the country, coupled with a failure to master the traditional techniques.

However, the deep-rooted art heritage still prevailed. In the early decades of this era it brought out several well-known painters, among them Ch'en Shih-ts'eng, Wu Ch'ang shih, and Wang I-t'ing, followed up by Ch'i Pei-Shih, Hsü Pei-hung and P'u Hsin-yü, Wu Ch'ang-shih and Chi Pei-Shih in particular have been well-known for their versatility in poetry, calligraphy, painting, and seal-engraving. Both of these artists had a drive and resilience that might have paved the way for art innovation. In the case of Ch'i Pei-Shih, the only regret is for his inadequate pursuit of literature, which was not on a par with his artistic achievements, otherwise he might claim a place with Matisse or Picasso.

With Chinese graphic art is Western painting, primarily divided into the academic and the unrealistic schools. Although history has proved the academic school a failure, Chinese artists have long been pursuing realistic Western painting. Among them notably we find these names: Tseng Po-ch'en of the Ming Dynasty, and Hsü Pei-Hung of the Republic. None of them went beyond pedantic imitation. Therefore even at their best they were able to claim places only as craftsmen. The latest painting styles of the Soviet Union are horrible, and their failure can be predicted. The unrealistic school of Western painting, pursuing the same route as Chinese artists in stressing rhythmic vitality rather than accuracy in details, bids well to be a success.

At present, the emphasis still falls on idealism, or the "Southern School". A fine future lies ahead for followers of this school and of Western painting in the Chinese tradition. Paintings in these two categories are finding their way overseas, particularly to places like Paris, New York, and Hongkong, where they are always received with enthusiasm. Hongkong is a place where many talented Chinese painters have congregated. Provided with beautiful surroundings and able to enjoy freedom of thought, Chinese artists living there have found an asylum to prepare for an eventual renaissance.

CONTEMPORARY INDIAN PAINTING

by RICHARD BARTHOLOMEW

Contemporary Indian painting is primarily expressionistic. And this is in keeping with the best traditions in Indian art. There is still much that is derivative. The transitional phase, however, has ended. The tentative, experimental and exploratory tendencies are now resolved. The exuberance and fire of an intensely catalytic period—the strong reaction from 1940 to 1950 against the pseudo-classicism of the Bengal School, principally revivalist—has cooled down.

Two factors prompted this reaction: the need for a new sensibility coupled to the need for a medium that would express this sensibility. The result has been the evolution of expressionism, and the emergence of oils as the principal medium.

Indian painters have had to resolve a strange dilemma. It was imperative that the European technique that they had learnt be fused with the indigenous vision. Essentially a figurative art, Indian art draws its images both from the village and from the city. In Indian painting today one sees the influence of folk iconography and of traditional motifs. While these can be powerful symbols in the hands of a genuine painter, however, they are no better than commercial signs in the work of the imitator. Incidentally, the reaction has also precipitated obnoxious byproducts—lame, inert paintings with fractured images. But this was inevitable in the first phase of a new school.

Besides those who affect modernism by way of the short cut there are some authentic deviationists. These are a few cubists; and there are the extreme expressionists whose work (abstract expressionism) sometimes verges on surrealism. There are also a few conscientious practitioners of abstract art, those who believe in pure art. But if there is a school of painting in India today it is expressionistic.

In this phase of introspection and of consolidation there are signs that a national idiom is emerging. With the change in the attitude to painting there has been a corresponding change in style, content, and purpose. Contemporary Indian painting, whatever its present defects may be, is no longer the effeminate, quasi-patriotic art that it was for the first four decades of this century when painters set out nostalgically to be Indian at any cost. The mask of sentiment has been cast off. Increasingly in recent years both easel painting and mural art have echoed the rhythm of the age.

The Characteristics of the New Painting

Drawing is boldly delineated. Brilliant colours, flatly applied or facetted with the palette-knife are juxtaposed daringly. The image is not amorphous but organic. Though economical, the drawing is fluid, stressing the cast of the eyes, the gesture of the hands and of the fingers. The mouth is eloquently depicted and the feet are stanced so as to suggest equilibrium or motion.

The expressionistic idiom, besides having won for itself an unchallenged supremacy, has an appreciative, if not consistently educated, following. There is no painter in India who is of an international calibre. And yet the best work of a dozen of our younger painters will command respect in any international show. There is nothing that is false if as yet there is nothing that is stupendous. The time is near at hand for the flowering of genius. With the state and the public interested in art, and with the climate of opinion energizing modern painting, it can be predicted that a national idiom will emerge, and with it genius.

The Roots of Expressionism

It is pertinent to find out why Indian painting today is expressionistic. A national idiom in the arts has to draw richly from the Indian psyche. It must receive its sustenance from the indigenous culture.

It is commonplace these days to say that India, and for that matter the East, is spiritual. This is a dangerous generalization. There is also the belief that Indians are an emotional people. This too is a dangerous generalization. All art, all great art that is to say, is spiritual. For art is the transformation of man's personal and collective experience—the humanistic spirit—into form. Animals which possess the lower ranges of the emotions do not create art. On the other hand primitive peoples have produced art that is pure and organic. Emotion, it must be remembered, and it cannot be stressed too often, is universal: otherwise art would not be universal.

In India an intricate religious system that encourages mysticism, pantheism, and varying degrees of transcendentalism, has consistently made allowances for the expression of extreme individualism. The liberation of the human spirit has been congruous to all Indian philosophical teaching. On the other hand an elaborate rationale justifying the social hierarchies (the caste system), and the ritualistic and patriarchial way of life (the joint family system), have contributed to the shaping of a quasi-introvert sensibility. These have been really intricate principles for the suppression of personality. The tropical sun, spiced diet and the dynamics of domestic history have subtly conditioned the Indian. On the surface the average Indian is effusive, generous and polite. But this is the facade that covers the turmoil of many

33

contradictions within. Indians are not a rational people. They have never been realistic. Idealism of one brand or another has conditioned politics and art. The past does not die easily in Indian culture and in Indian art.

Since the art of a period records the conscience of the period these qualities of prostration and of intense individuality—the qualities of discipline and of assertion—have gone into the making of Indian art. There has been assimilation and reformation. And this has resulted in a series of compressions. In philosophy, in religion, and in art, and later in politics, what is typically Indian has been characterized by a quality of compression. This instinct for compression has been formulated into an organic form in art. Indian music is melodic, not harmonic. It has expressionistic qualities whether it be instrumental or vocal. The Indian dance is symbolic. The movements, dynamically conceived, extend organically into space. The stances have sculpturesque qualities. The mimetic elements are accentuated. There is no place for formalistic flourishes in the Indian dance. Vigour is stressed rather than qualities of grace. In the Kathakali dance, for instance, mask, mime and symbolic choreography while simplifying the expression actually accentuates it. The same principle of accentuation is noticeable in Indian sculpture. Except for the decadent, all Indian sculpture has been expressionistic.

2

The Influence of World War II : The Reorientation in Attitude

The revolt against the revivalist tendencies of the Bengal School in the middle of the thirties was motivated by changes in education and in society. The impact of the West on India was the most intense and concentrated during the war period. World War II put values into the melting pot everywhere. It did the same in India. Very subtly the presence of hundreds of thousands of foreign troops in India affected the status quo of Indian society. The young of this generation met the young from other nations. Indian manpower was harnessed for the war effort. Education in technology and in the humanities received a great fillip. On the other hand war restrictions changed the face of Indian economics, modernizing and streamlining commerce and business.

The presence of a large heterogeneous element in the country, and the forces of the new education, helped to eradicate some of the old prejudices. The war effort and consequent employment bucked up the morale of the people. With this was the bid to achieve complete independence non-violently, a movement in which everybody participated spiritually. While practically the whole of Europe was at war, and two of the major countries of the East, Japan and China, were at war; when it seemed that spiritual values were being challenged all around him, the Indian artist perhaps unconsciously felt the need to preserve at home the humanistic values of a rich heritage in the arts.

The pressure exerted by the necessities of war brought a modern approach towards many problems. It modified our ways of thinking. The freedoms that the West tried to preserve at such great sacrifice, and the freedom that we as a nation were looking forward to, these were the inspiring banners under which this generation of painters grew up to maturity. If freedom was a uuiversal concept, and if the values which are inherent in freedom are universal, then art which was the supremest expression of these values was also universal. Great Indian art was no better nor worse than great European art. What was it that the West tried to preserve at such great cost? And what was it that the artists in India had to preserve?

Strangely enough the war created a new pragmatic attitude. It opened the doors of the West: ⟨and it made us spring-clean our own.⟩ Indian artists looked both ways, and there was much to learn from what they saw.

The Bengal School: Its Decadence

The decadence of the Bengal School stared painters in the face. Obviously there was a need for a new sensibility and for a regeneration. The medium of this school was wash. Their technique was effeminate. Except for the early masters like Abanindranath Tagore and Nandalal Bose who had used the medium with considerable sensitivity the followers of the Bengal School had dissipated the potentialities of tempera and wash. In their hands the wash technique had become sentimental and mawkish. Drawing had lost vitality. The Kangra and Ajanta styles which at the start this school tried to emulate, had become mere pastiche. The Bengal School had come to a dead end. It had become an art of escape.

The reasons for the decadence were obvious. A pseudo-romanticism had blighted much of the work of the followers of the Bengal School. Decorative tendencies crept in. These imitators missed the intense lyricism of the Kangra painters. There was something dogmatic and archaic about their work. The painters of the later Bengal School mistook the pretty and the decorative for the beautiful and the dynamic. There was far too much of sentiment and too little of emotion. Form, as conceived by them, was not organic. They did not appreciate that a religious art at Ajanta, the product of emotion recollected in tranquillity, could not be transferred literally to an age increasingly conditioned by the rhythm of machinery and the tempo of urban life. With preponderant literary themes for their content they tried to make an art out of patience, application and a mis-directed search for an aesthetic emotion which they thought would be typically Indian. They painted languid-eyed females with sweeping drapery who stood at wells or under blasted trees. These wistful and sentimentally conceived images of men and women were placed on the shores of impossible seas. The banks of rivers or a hazy landscape attempted to set off the poetic attitude. The images of slender gods and goddesses in the eternal twilight of the Bengal School glow were anachronisms in the age of pin-ups, the cinema and fabrics with machine design. The old mythology was no longer functional, and the age did not want romanticism of that brand.

Was this, the Indian painters asked themselves, the culmination of twenty-five centuries of Indian art? And was it consonant with art the world over?

There was the need to look for tradition all over again. The Bengal School initiated by Abanindranath Tagore and Harvell, having taken inspiration from Ajanta, and some of the Kangra painters, had petered out.

Its condition in the forties is best described by these words from Keats:
"Thou art a dreaming thing, a fever of thyself."

3

The Search for an Intrinsic Tradition

True, the West had a lot to teach in technique. But for an expression
of the Indian sensibility the aesthetic endeavour would have to be rooted
in tradition. Before discussing what the moderns have learnt from the West,
and what use they have made of it, let us reconstruct the "re-discovery"
of tradition. If we examine some of the salient characteristics of Indian art
we will realize what indigenous tradition really means to the contemporary
Indian painter. There are evidences of an organic sensibility as far back
as the Mohenjo-Daro civilization (2000–3000 B.C.). In some of the seals
discovered from excavations at Mohenjo-Daro the bas-relief pictographs of
animals, the animal images and the hieroglyphics constitute a complete unit
of aesthetic expression.

Whether we examine the bas-relief of the temple sculpture, or the ancient
seals, or the frescoes in Ajanta and Ellora, there is one characteristic of the
imagination which is a constant. This is the Indian artist's power to visualize the image dynamically. Because of this Indian art has never been florid
or decorative or representational though time and again, in the decadent
phases, there have been decorative tendencies. The element of compression,
and of symbolic simplification, is evidence of an expressionistic form.

The dynamic way the Indian artist organized space is manifest in all
periods of Indian art. The corollary to this is the use of the flexed, ambient
line. The line encloses space, and the line suggests space. Voluminous proportions, therefore, have to be very exact. For instance, the sculptural
friezes that depict the Durga-Mahisamardini at the Vaital Deul Temple at
Puri, and the detail from the wheel at Konarak (a St. George and the Dragon
motif) have the emotive qualities and the form of compression similar to
that in the seals.

The same organic principle contacts much of the surviving sculpture.
It is apparent in the sculpture of the Buddhist period. We have but to
look at some of the samples of relievo-work in the museums that embody
all the distinguishing features of Indian sculpture at its best. We see these
features in the "Inscribed Railing Pillar". The lovely carved bull on this
stone still communicates the vitality and the rhythm the early sculptor saw
in the animal. "The Mahaparinirvana Scene," "The Birth of Jyotishka"
and "Buddha and the Jatilas" are exquisite pieces of carving in which every
inch of available space on the stone has been made articulate. The same
elements are apparent in the Amaravati and Goli friezes depicting anecdotes
from the life of the Buddha.

Similarly in the better-known Nataraj statue depicting the dance of
Shiva, who is Creator, Preserver and Destroyer (really a cosmic concept) the
expressionistic idiom is seen in its perfection. The very concept of Limgam
worship is an expressionistic attitude. This archetypal form has gone into
the stupas, of temples and of pagodas. It denotes the power of ascension

symbolic of man's creative aspirations. For the spirit of man in the most intimate of intercourses, without in any sense being vulgar, is compressed and transformed and impressed upon another. This brings us to the magnificient sculpture at Khajuraho. Far from being erotic the sculpture at Khajuraho sanctifies physical beauty and physical love. Many of the sculptures of the Jain period exemplify the body beautiful.

If a linear representation of these sculptures were made the drawings would still be art for the dynamic line still communicates the compressed feeling. Again if we look at the Jain murals at Kanchipuram, and at the illuminated work of the Gujarati Kalpa Sutra, we find evidences of an economical design and a form of compression which accentuates the image while investing it with symbolic qualities. In these examples of sculpture, painting and design there are no formalistic traits.

Much has been said of the beauties of Ajanta. But the contemporary painter, though he may admire the great imagination that conceived it, sees in Ajanta a sensibility that does not correspond with the particular sensitivity of the age he lives in. And similarly, the lyricism and the delicate tonal harmonies of the Pahari painters offer him neither the form nor the technique with which he could express his sensibility. Therefore, for his artistic ancestry and for vital stimulation he went to the Indian sources mentioned— to Indian sculpture, specimens of which can still be seen, to the Indian dance and Indian music, still vitally practised today, and of course back to the living folk traditions in the villages.

The Four Pioneers of Modern Indian Painting

The revolt against the Bengal School, though it was not a concerted movement, finally culminated in the discovery of traditional expressionism. The new movement that originated from Bombay was born at a time when expressionism was in vogue in Europe. It was Van Gogh and Rouault and Paul Klee and Modigliani, primarily expressionist painters, and not so much Picasso and Braque and Matisse, who inspired the Indian painters of the forties to paint as they did.

But the painters of the forties had their immediate antecedents in India as well. These were the pioneers who indicated the possibilities of painting in oils. Amrita Sher Gil and Sailoz Mookherjea and Jamini Roy, in the earlier phase, all worked in oils. Each presented a different vision of India. Amrita Sher Gil and Sailoz Mookherjea learnt their technique abroad. Having seen at first hand the aesthetic ferment in Europe these two painters returned to India to evolve characteristic styles of their own.

At first influenced by Gauguin Amrita Sher Gil ultimately incorporated the lyrical element that distinguishes Kangra painting. She achieved in oils what the Pahari painters had done in tempera. She painted the India that she saw around her, without embellishment.

These pensively stanced figures of the countryside in a Sher Gil painting breathe a romanticism that is born of the regret that these things were passing away. In "The Bramacharis", for instance, and in "Siesta" and

"Elephant Promenade" the drawing and the colouring are intrinsically her own. These great and eloquent paintings portray all that is eternal in India, the mood of the quiet landscape, the character of her people, their simple ways, their calm acceptance of life. More than any other modern painter before her Amrita Sher Gil orientated the Indian sensibility to the use of oils.

Sailoz Mookherjea, another pioneer, attempted to fuse together the fluid technique in oils with the characteristically Indian attitude to nature. In such compositions as "Washing Day", "Wind" and "Harvest" one sees the influence of Matisse in the drawing—reinforced by colours that are vibrant and Indian. By the end of the forties Mookherjea had simplified the style of the Pahari school evolving a lyrical style that was eminently suited to oils, and to his sensibility. His theme was the pastoral landscape—the magnificent sweep of land and sky, and people toiling or resting in the brilliance of an Indian glow.

Jamini Roy, who found his motifs in folk toys and in rural art, introduced primitivism into Indian painting. He brought in a Byzantine sensibility, and expressionistic traits are again prominent. There is stress on design, on the vitality of the line and on brilliant colours cleverly, and daringly, juxtaposed. Religious themes, Indian and Christian, feature in Jamini Roy's art. At his best in the linear compositions which are reminiscent of the grouping and the stresses of sculptural friezes Jamini Roy's art has a simple vitality that is impressive and refreshing. But having introduced a vital form into painting Jamini Roy repeated himself and became facile. Unfortunately, he has not developed.

Among the precursors of Indian expressionism must be numbered the poet Tagore. Strangely enough what seemed mere doodlings of a dreamer and a versatile genius, turned out to be a vivid form of metaphysical painting by the time the pieces came to be collected and exhibited a decade after the poet's death. Like Munch's work but with a visionary splendour reminiscent of Blake's, the still terror and the mysterious character of these doodlings have made Indian painters realize that expressionism, an intuitive principle, was fundamentally Indian. They realized also that the stream of Indian painting would have been different if this corollary to the poet's genius had been taken seriously some twenty-five years ago.

5

The Bombay School: Its Characteristics

The nucleus of the New Painting is in Bombay. The greater body of efficient and experimental painters reside there. Bombay is the home of M. F. Husain (*Color Pl. 2*), Mohan Samant (*Pl. 17*), R. D. Raval, Akbar Padamsee, Newton Souza, Tayeb Mehta, Hebber, Chavda (*Pl. 20*), Gade and Gaitonde (*Pl. 18*).

In Delhi, the capital, there is the second vital assembly of painters. Ram Kumar (*Pl. 25*), Satish Gujral (*Pl. 24*), Biren De, Amina Ahmed (*Pl. 23*), Kanwal Krishna and K. S. Kulkarni are the principal Delhi painters. Krishen Khanna (*Pl. 26*), a promising young painter, once closely associated with the Bombay group, is now in Madras. Jamini Roy is still working in Calcutta;

and Ram Kinkar, now better known as a teacher than as a painter, is at Shantinekatan.

In Indian expressionist painting there are two major divisions. There are the painters who use the image of man to communicate their attitude to life. The image of man, for them, is the most eloquent of forms. Man for them is a metaphor. The predicament of man in the city; the perpetual martyrdom of man in the effort to preserve values; man in conflict or man enmeshed in his own emotions; man oppressed by man, and man resurgent —in fact, man in all the moods of life, tender, terrible, and troubled—these are themes for some painters. Man is the principal theme for Husain, Ram Kumar, Satish Gujral, Krishen Khanna, Akbar Padamsee and Mohan Samant, to name the most significant of the painters in whose work dramatic (and sometimes epic) qualities are evident. Nature for them is man.

On the other hand painters such as Biren De, Kulkarni, Hebber, Chavda, Gade, Raval, and Sailoz Mookherjea portray man in his relation to his environment. The figures are part of a general scheme, and the stress is on compositional values. Without being landscape painters they use the landscape or the locale to reinforce the mood. These are primarily lyrical paintings and by and large they have been influenced by the beauties of Pahari painting. Such pictures are modern versions of the Indian painter's poetic approach to nature. This is the new pastoralism, pastoralism because the content has been drawn from outside the city. However, this does not imply that the mood is calm, or idyllic or nostalgic. In between these two categories are the abstractionists, few in number, but faithful to their vision. The rhythm of colour and line, pattern and texture, characterize the work of Amina Ahmed, Gaitonde and, more recently, Mohan Samant.

I have classified the painters so as to indicate something of the content. Naturally, no significant painter is rigid or limited in his scope. Husain, for instance, and Samant have produced work which could be classified in all three categories. Gujral has propensities for the surrealistic; Ram Kumar is developing a fantastic idiom reminiscent of Chagall's. Ara, working in water colours, can turn out a delightful still-life. Kanwal Krishna, with the same medium, but with the addition of dope, Indian ink, and erasures with a blade and bits of glass produces sublimated scenes of snow, the Himalayas, icebergs and emotive versions of the crucifixion.

There has been a change in attitude towards painting. From depicting the obviously Indian spectacle (Hebber's dancers, for example, and Chavda's coolies) painters have come to portray the subtler characteristics of India. The obvious adaptations of Van Gogh's cyclo-chromatic technique, his manner of variegating the surface and of illuminating an area with a militant colour—these were discoveries put to good use very early in the forties. But as the years passed there was a conscientious attempt to be less derivative and more organic in technique. Style is the mastery of technique. The modern Indian painter working in oils is resourceful. He concentrates on the image, the colour scheme and the tactile effect. To fuse these elements together he depends on these technical aids: palette-knife inscriptions; bold drawing and brushwork; impasto; facetted colour; textures; figure outlines; false perspective and counterpointed colour.

By the time one comes to "Zameen" (The Land), the magnum opus of the most significant living painter, we see that the approach to painting has changed. Husain's "Zameen" brings us to the work of the leaders of the expressionist movement in India. If we analyze the work of Husain, Ram Kumar, Satish Gujral and Mohan Samant we shall see the best there is in Indian painting today.

M. F. Husain: The Symbolism of "Zameen"

The outstanding painter of this generation is unmistakably Husain. Once a sign-board painter, he is completely self-taught and as such he is not cramped by academic formalism and obtuse theories of painting. In his work the elements of traditional expressionism are the most eloquent. Husain is a great draughtsman, a subtle colourist, a conscientious experimenter and a purist in technique. His influence on the younger generation is apparent. The use he has made of the human figure, and of the images of rural life, his periodic essays into differentiating form, have been stimulating examples of original endeavour.

Though "Zameen" is a large painting there is an organic life of colour and design that animates it. The painting is like a symphony in five movements. Like Urdu calligraphy it is to be read from left to right. The first section depicts a drummer and four animated figures standing beside a tree. Over them all shines an elemental (perhaps harvest) moon. The song, dance and the air of festivity represent leisure, recreation and passion. Below this section, like a key to it, is the image of an arm with a fish incorporated in it. This image symbolizes fertility. The second section depicts interiors. There is a mother and child motif in the top half, and a woman churning in the lower. In the marginal fringe we see an arrangement of pots. Houses in the background fill up something of the upper space. As they move in from the first section to the second they knit together the two.

The central section, the third, very vividly and violently coloured, depicts the gods and the religious beliefs of the village folk. The yellow figure of the priest forms the key to this section.

The fourth and fifth sections are correlatives to what has preceded. Two bulls in arrangements of blue and yellow, and a man constructed similarly, reveal to us the power behind human and animal effort. Nature, the sunshine, the water, and the earth are represented with yellow, blue and brown. These colours symbolize environmental fertility.

The fifth panel, the last, is fragmented. The total power of the painting has now been resolved into what is an epilogue. We see village literacy work, blossoms, a woman sifting the grain, a pack mule, a crowing cock and a paper-kite fluttering. Thrown superbly together these images, without any rational endeavour, reconstruct the village scene. There are no indications of flourish or of a false finesse. The strength lies in the simplicity of the vision; and yet Husain has been able to suggest the diversity behind the design of village life.

Ram Kumar: The People and Their Problems

In the work of Ram Kumar we see a different sensibility and consequently a different subject matter. The pictorial language has changed and with it the imagery. Since he is a novelist and essayist in Hindi, besides a painter, there is a literary motive in Ram Kumar's work which is cleverly disguised. He is essentially a painter who portrays the "still, sad music of humanity". The dramatis personae in the social predicament that he depicts stand naively in the foreground (as do the figures in child art and in primitive drawing). These are stanced eloquently against a mechanistic cityscape which has been rendered into a neutral geometry. In his work we see a tragic propensity. The enlarged eyes, intensely illuminated and often squint, perhaps symbolic of cross-purposes, conflict and self-interrogation, the eloquent gesture of the hand, raised to signal or in an endeavour at self-protection, the method of thrusting the protagonist into the foreground (as though he or she were delivering a soliloquy) are all characteristic features of this painter's style. They are forms of accentuation.

In paintings such as "Sad Town" and "Night" the marionette-like figures, suspended before the next act, convey a sense of arrested animation. The few lamps in the street and the taut electric wires denote the insular energy that surrounds these spiritually destitute and tormented people. More recently, in "A Street in Paris" and "A Town in Hungary" the symbols of the church and of the café are cleverly deployed. A woman frozen indeterminately between the café and the street, and a man with his back to the church and the icy mountains suggest the element of flight in the lives of these people, if not the ways of escape. A tender quality of compassion, more psychological than religious, articulates the theme without making it melodramatic.

Satish Gujral: The Mortal Coil

Satish Gujral, a keen admirer of the Mexican school, is another powerful painter. When influences on the younger painters have been mainly European, he has brought in fresh blood. He has an individual myth, and something of a prophetic zeal. He is the portrayer of a humanity that is outraged by violence, oppression and the devices of the unscrupulous and the cruel. His paintings interpret the temper of the times. For instance, in "Snare of Memories" we see man struggling against himself and the conflicts within him. Or we see man struggling heroically against his oppressors as in "Despair".

If there is an element of phantasmagoria in the work of Ram Kumar which voices a still terror, in the paintings of Satish Gujral one sees a macabresque quality of primeval ritual. There is no sophistication in this direct and dynamic portrayal. A sense of volume inherent in each painting impresses itself on the spectator. And even if the painting is not his cup of tea, he has to accept the premise of the painting, and admit its power. In "Desolation" the vortex of the movement draws the eye on to the tragic figure and then on to the rudimentary environment. The corded noose beside the figure, and the cold volcanic cone in the background, grow intergrally out of the composition like the perfect sequence of a dream.

Gujral has a surrealistic predilection. Quite often he employs the elements of condensation and of displacement to create the authentic mood of a dream. What is infinitely more startling, and effective, is the unusual tints which highlight and diversify an otherwise sombre palette.

When the form of symbolism is more integral, we have, as in that brilliant portrait of Mr. Nehru, a painting which is poignantly haunting. The red jacket and the blue rose which Mr. Nehru wears are symbolic; and his extended arms and clasped hands are significant gestures. The hook-and-claw contrivance in the background, dangling like a bait which the Prime Minister [ignores, adds piquancy to the portrait without making it over-literal. In this portrait of Mr. Nehru we see the crusader and the idealist, the saint and the martyr, the publicman and the visionary. The portrait is essentially the portrait of a leader, looking before and after.

Mohan Samant: Incantation in Painting

Intensely interested in music, and consequently now in an abstract phase, Mohan Samant was once an intense expressionist. Even in his earliest work a quality of mysticism was evident. His lurid colours—the flaming reds, the absorbent violets and ultramarines, and the unflinching greens in his painting "Sleepless Night"—are all shot with an apocalyptical vision. There is a Rouault-like incandescence in Samant's work. Colour is employed emotively, and most of Samant's paintings vibrate. One word best describes these paintings—incantation.

If the colours are prismatic the spectacle is equally startling. The painting, "Broken Mirrors", has for its remarkable design a nude in a room of shattered mirrors. The multiple reflections of the same image repeat the motif differently. And the change in size, perspective and colour transforms a simple phenomenon into a metaphysical experience. The same effect is subtly varied in the painting "Lovers in the Palanquin". A night of the intensest blue, and the processional grouping of the figures, transform an idyllic motif into a surprising spectacle wherein reality overlaps the dream.

Samant, one can only hope, has not gone irrevocably the way of abstraction. The present phase was inevitable for the restless spirit of this adventurous painter. The fire and zeal of the old Byzantine artists was in him and a religious dedication to the task of extending the limits of painting. The colder metaphysics of the abstract phase, I hope, will not extinguish irreparably the poet, the lover and the lunatic in him.

The work of these four painters represent the best that there is in Indian expressionism. Samant and Husain know the way into the abstractionist camp; Gujral is at present toying with surrealism, and the immense possibilities of mural art; Ram Kumar, as I have said before, is on the verge of a magical view of the world, ready to leave behind emotion for ecstasy and bliss.

One is tempted to read significances into these interesting painters and their work. What is apparent, however, is that these are dedicated painters, humble before the dictates of their technique, and of their experience. They know that to pervert either would be to sully the image.

Indian painting is young. The best that I can say for our painters is that they look upon the world, and into themselves, with the positive eyes of discovery.

A SHORT HISTORY OF INDONESIAN ART

by KUSNADI

The history of Indonesian Art can be considered to begin with sarcophagi dating from the Neolithic Period, between 2000 and 1500 B.C. Symbolic sculpture of a very primitive technique reflects the culture of our ancestors.

A first step in the development from a primitive to what may be termed a "classic" era (classic in the sense that certain techniques and style are of a high standard in almost all branches of art) is to be seen in houses built by newcomers from Indo-China, which they decorated with wood carvings.

A second step was the acceptance of Hindu art from India soon after the first contacts between Indonesia and India in the first century A.D. The art which then came into being is called Hindu-Indonesian art.

The nature of the monuments dating from that period differs in each region, since each region had its own characteristic and abilities. The remnants of Çriwidjaja architecture in Sumatra differ from the temples in Java, e.g., the Buddhistic stupa of Borobudur (750 A.D.) and the Sjiwaistic Prombanan temples (900 A.D.). They likewise differ from the Panataran temples in East Java and from the "Pura" of Bali. Sumatran architecture is ornamental rather than monumental; on the other hand Central Javanese architecture is more monumental in appearance, while that in Bail is both monumental and ornamental.

The wooden architecture which developed later with its fine carvings reflects certain characteristics of such stone temples as those of Tjeribon and Bali, and reflects too something of the Chinese style, generally conducive to the development of a dynamic art. The Indian element on the contrary embodies a serene character. This wooden architecture is to be found on almost all the islands; on Sumatra in the Batak and Minangkabau regions, on Java in Tjeribon, Pekalongan, Jogiakarta, Surakarta and Japara, and on Bali, Barneo, Celebes, and Timor.

Besides carving there exists the art of decorative weaving in many of the above regions, together with the art of batik, which manifests itself only in Java.

The so-called "wayang kerutjil" of wood and leather grew from a desire to personify characters in pure native literature. Next came the "wayang bèbèr," paintings on cloth depicting fragments of stories. In West Java the "wayang golèk" came into being to give form to Indian stories from classic literature, while in Central-Java it depicts Arabic stories imported by the first Moslems. And as the direct result too of the acceptance of classic literature from India—Mahabarata and Ramayana—the "wayang kulit" (leather wayang puppets) came into being in Surakarta, Jogjakarta and Bali.

The Balinese puppets depict characters from the Ramayana in the form and style of temple reliefs, and represent people in a manner which is both expressive and decorative and yet realistic. The leather puppets of Java on the contrary underwent a series of stylizations, so that in the end they only show a very slight resemblance to real people. A great skill in leather chiselling makes the puppet a highly intricate a-jour product, minutely perforated and yet unified. Gorgeous colours and gold make it a piece of delicate art.

In Bali, the realistic puppet gives rise to drawing on cloth or paper. This in turn produces the desire to depict other stories, based on the painter's own imagination and his natural surroundings, or family and outdoor life. The art of wayangs has been a source of free inspiration in Bali down to today.

Sculpture makes use of many media in Bali: ivory, hard wood, soft wood, and porous stone. The Stylization of natural forms into others imbued by a spirit of freedom, expressive yet subtle, has become a characteristic of Balinese art. Frogs, birds, fish, deer, fragments of some story or other, are carved in their respective splendours with a skill that seems to defy the technical difficulties inherent in hard materials.

Another art occurring on many islands is the making of masks which are used in the dance and the drama.

Raden Saleh Bustaman was the first painter who had the opportunity of studying in Europe, through the good offices of the Dutch painter Payen in the colonial era. It was undoubtedly Raden Saleh with his outstanding talents who quietly led the younger generation to paint in the new manner. Of all his paintings "The Wild Bull and Tiger in the Blazing Forest" is the most popular. This painting is becoming more widely known, especially since the wild bull has been adopted as the symbol of national strength. Two of his paintings can be seen in the Jakarta Museum. Others are in the Jogja court, representing members of the Sultan's family, and two others in the Mangkunegaran court depict lions. Raden Saleh's art is not different from Renaissance art in Europe, especially from the last period, Romanticism, and most typically, Delacroix (1799–1863). Raden Saleh's art is naturalism in the sense that his paintings are faithful representations of reality in form, colour and perspective.

Next come Abdullah and Wakidi, separated from Raden Saleh by rather a long interval. Both have a marked fondness for depicting beautiful landscapes with mountains and ricefields naturalistically.

Better known is Abdullah's son, Basuki Abdullah, who is a graduate of a Dutch academy. He prefers painting people to painting landscapes, but he shows the human soul only very superficially. The name that follows is that of S. Sudjojono, who managed to unite the first painters in an association called "Persatuan Ahli Gambar Indonesia" (Persagi) at Djakarta in 1937.

He received his first training from Pirngadi and the Japanese painter Yazaki. He was very much inspired by reproductions of painting by Van Gogh, the pioneer of expressionism, who strengthened his belief that superficial romantic art, such as was produced by Basuki Abdullah or by the Dutch "Tourist-painters" Dezentje and Adolfs, should be condemned.

With the cooperation of Agus Djayasuminta, he formed the "Persagi" and succeeded in producing a new, characteristically Indonesian style with a free technique and a soul of its own.

Before 1942—Uuder Dutch Rule.

During the period of colonial government the art of painting or rather art in general—the development of the sense of beauty—did not have a place in the minds of the people. The people did not know yet the meaning of art as one of the three main branches of culture:

1. *Philosophy and religion, which determine our views in life.*
2. *Science as a means of achieving a practical way of life.*
3. *Art, which develops man's sense of beauty, bringing forth ideals of creation and perfection.*

1942–1945—The Japanese Occupation.

The group of painters grew, with young artists from other places choosing Jakarta as the centre for their training under the guidance of the masters mentioned above.

The Japanese Government welcomed this growth of painting and fostered the hope that it might be of great help towards the realization of cultural ideals. With this end in view they set up a Cultural Office—"Keimin Bunka Shidōsho"—headed by Japanese artists. "Putra" (an organization for the concentration of the people's forces), while fighting for the people's rights and welfare under Sukarno, Hatta, Ki Hadjar Dewantara and Kijai Hadji Mansur, did not forget to stimulate the growth of art in Indonesia and to see that art was not used for purposes of Japanese propaganda.

Under the auspices of the Japanese Cultural Office exhibitions were held not only in Jakarta but in othert owns as well. Meanwhile "Putra" did not remain idle. To keep the two sides of the scale balanced, exhibitions were regularly held by Putra's Art Department under Sudjojono and Affandi (*Pl. 27*).

This was the time when Otto Djajasuminta, Kartono Yudhokusumo (*Pl. 33*), Henk Ngantung, Emiria Sunassa and quite a number of other young painters made their first appearance in the Indonesian art world.

After 1945.

Because at the beginning of the revolution there was no security and peace in Jakarta, nearly all Indonesian painters left the big city for quiet Jogjakarta, which was the capital of the Republic until 1950.

A new painters' group under the name of "Seniman Indonesia Muda" (Young Indonesian Artists' Society) was formed by Sudjojono in 1946.

In 1947, to open new ways to the younger generation, a society was formed by Hendra with the name "Pelukis Rakjat" (People's Artists).

With the birth of the "Pelukis Rakjat" the way was open for a new branch of the fine arts, sculpture, which had been initiated by Affandi as early as 1943. In the first stages the sculptors used clay as their material. The first carving in stone was done by Hendra, and the first exhibition of sculpture was held in 1948.

In 1950 a new society, "Pelukis Indonesia" (The Indonesian Painters' Society), was formed. A number of "Pelukis Rakjat" members joined the new group. Their president was Sumitro, later Sholihin.

Another painters' group, lead by Djajengasmoro, is the "Pusat Tenaga Pelukis Indonesia", formed by a number of artists in Jogjakarta before "Seniman Indonesia Muda" was organized.

The year 1952 saw the birth of yet another club—the "Pelukis Indonesia Muda" (Young Indonesian Painters' Society), led by Widajat (Pl. 30). This group consists of students and ex-students of the Academy of Arts in Jogjakarta.

Academy "Seni Rupa Indonesia" (ASRI).

The ASRI (Academy of Arts) in Jogjakarta was founded by the Ministry of Education in 1950 with Katamsi as its director. The teachers were recruited from the artists' clubs mentioned above.

Other Towns.

In Jakarta is the "Gabungan Pelukis Indonesia", founded in 1948, with Sutiksna as president. Bandung has "Jiva Mukti," founded in 1948 by Barli; "Tjipta Pantjaran Rasa" was formed in 1953 by Abedy; the "Sanggar Seniman" was formed in 1952 by Kartono Yudhokusumo.

At the Technical Faculty in Bandung is an institute for the training of drawing-masters under the directorship since 1950, of S. Sumardja. He is assisted by the Dutch painter Ries Mulder.

In Surakarta was the "Pelangi" (1947–1949) with Sularko as president, and there's now the "Himpunan Budaya Surakarta," formed by Dr. Murdowo.

In Madium there is the "Tunas Muda", first under Kartono, later under Sunindyo.

In Sarabaja there is the "Prabangkara" founded in 1952, under the leadership of Karyono Js. In Malang is the "Angkatan Pelukis Muda Malang" with Widagdo as chairman. In Bukittinggi (Central Sumatra) is the "Seniman Muda Indonesia" (SEMI), under the leadership of Zetka.

In Medan (East Sumatra) there is the "Angkatan Seni Rupa Indonesia" (1945) led by Ismail Daulay. The "Seniman Merdeka" is a younger club under the leadership of Dr. Djulham. In Palembang (South Sumatra) is a group of students under the guidance of Mohammad Saleh.

At Ubud (Bali) is a group of Balinese painters with Anak Agung Gde Sobrat as president (*Color Pl. 3*).

Art Movements or Schools—Their Salient Features.

To enjoy works of fine art in general, and painting in particular, it is of the greatest importance to pay attention to various schools, characteristics, or "isms," to their individual attractions, functions, and aims.

Primitive Characteristics.

The primitive existed in the first simple forms of culture and still prevails among backward peoples and among children. Such is the case too in isolated villages and regions of Indonesia, the form being "kuda képang" or "kuda lumping" in Java and Sumatra respectively, with very simple or childish colour composition and shape.

Naturalism.

The purpose of this style or school is the creation of artefacts resembling natural form, perspective and colour as much as possible.

In painting, this style was seriously begun by the painters of the Italian Renaissance in the 15th Century. The whole of Europe followed this school until the middle of the 19th Century, while Western academic studies were based exclusively on it.

It was with Raden Saleh that this school first began to be known in Indonesia. Contemporary painters such as Trubus in oil and Sunarto **Pr.** in pastel drawing are good examples.

Impressionism.

Western painters were leaving naturalism for a more clear-cut atmosphere and movement than naturalism. The Easterner on the other hand never based his art on naturalism. The Easterner experiences rather the conciousness of nature's force and motion before attempting to paint.

In what is called "impressionistic", the dynamic or vague, in some cases touching the realistic or abstract, Western and the Eastern works are the same. It is understandable that Japanese art helped "impressionism" in Paris and this in turn was to be a stimulus in the development of a new art in Indonesia when "Persagi" was born. Sholihin for example is a good impressionist.

Expressionism.

An expressionist painter paints the psyche or the "soul" of his subject, not merely the exterior or environment.

Feelings of relief or liberation are expressed freely. The East has long preserved this element, even basing its art on it. Thus there are primitive arts alive in their decorative lines and colours. It was after Raden Saleh that "Expressionism" was born in Indonesia, out of naturalistic portrait art, just as in the West. Affandi's paintings have lately been based on expressionism.

Modern Schools.

In the modern school the painter becomes a composer—a real creator, no more an instrumentalist or singer of someone else's song! He is a long way from naturalistic art bound to natural forms.

Beauty of colour has become really important; proportions and forms are designed according to new views, while imagination and musicality are decisive elements.

Salim in Paris is one of our foremost modernists.

In Indonesia signs of modernity are to be noted in colouring, as in Nasjah's latest works, and in the compositions of the painters Zaini, Rusli and Osman Effendi. Such signs of progress are on the whole not yet free from the older expressionism. They are clearer, however, in the linear compositions of Sadali or But Mochtar (*Pl. 34*) and in recent sculptures of Arby.

Note:

This short history of Indonesian art is an extract with some changes from the article by the same author in "Indonesian Art", published by the Art Department of the Cultural Office, Ministry of Education and Culture (1955)

THE ART OF JAPAN
by MICHIAKI KAWAKITA

Even in the wide field of Asian art, the art of Japan occupies a special position. From ancient times it has been an art with a brightness and a gentleness all its own. We may begin with geographic characteristics: the Japanese islands lie in an arc to the east of Asia, and, since they are near the continent, the various cultures that have developed there have each in turn flowed in. The nature of the country and the people has been such that each successive flow has been welcomed. Artistic movements of all sorts have been preserved, and, in the hotbed that is Japan, something quite new and different has grown up. It was to this situation that the Meiji critic Okakura Tenshin referred when he boasted: "Japan is a museum for the art of Asia; and as a living and working museum, it is indeed something more than a museum."

If we look at Japanese art in a very general way, we may divide it into four periods:

I: Archaic
1. Neolithic Age (to 100 B.C.)
2. Bronze Age (200 B.C.—250 A.D.)
3. Age of the Burial Mounds(250—551)

II: Classical
4. Asuka Period (552—644)
5. Nara Period (645—793)
6. Heian Period (794—1185)
7. Kamakura Period (1186—1338)

III. Near-modern
8. Muromachi Period (1339—1574)
9. Momoyama Period (1575—1614)
10. Edo Period (1615—1867)

IV: Modern
  11. Early Modern (1868—1945)
  12. Contemporary (1945—   )

I: The archaic era, covering a thousand to two thousand years down to the introduction of Buddhism in the mid-sixth century, includes the Neolithic Age, the Bronze Age, and the Age of the Burial Mounds. We know of its art only through excavations, and ideed its products are perhaps too primitive to be called art at all. Yet the general outlines of Japanese art are already apparent, and formal and aesthetic characteristics to become clear only later are already present in a direct, intuitive manner. Since most of the findings call up associations with the cultures of the continent, moreover, we may conclude that from an early age Japanese culture developed side by side with those cultures.

Among objects that call for attention in the Neolithic Age are the Jômon or "Rope-pattern" earthenware utensils and images, which reveal a primitive energy and a powerful will toward form. Next come the Yayoi earthenware utensils, in which a sense of the gentle and the bright becomes clearer, and a considerable growth toward disciplined form is to be noted. Bronze swords and spears also appear, indicating that the Bronze Age has arrived from the continent. The most remarkable bronze objects are the bells called *dôtaku*, not to be found on the continent. The *dôtaku* in a sense pioneer the way to a simple, generous sense of form that is the special characteristic of Japanese art. By the Age of the Burial Mounds, we are in historical times. Among the relics are mirrors, swords, armor, and other personal accessories, all suggesting the continent in conception and execution, and all showing remarkable progress over earlier artifacts. Special mention must be made of the *haniwa* earthen images. We may perhaps say that in their simplicity, freedom, and approachability, they display the formal sense of the Japanese at its most classical.

We thus see that in the rough surroundings of the archaic ages something which we may consider the original mold of Japanese art was given simple expression. Although it has much in common with primitive art everywhere, it shows a certain simplicity, cleanness, and gentleness of its own. In particular, one notes a very special flavor in a softness of emotional connotation and in a mildness and moderation not to be found on the continent. The art of succeeding periods is the application of this initial mold to changing circumstances.

II: The classical era, our second general category, centers upon the Buddhist art that came with the introduction of that religion. It includes the lively periods from the mid-sixth century to the fourteenth century: Asuka, Nara, Heian, and Kamakura.

In the Asuka Period, Buddhism arrived from the continent. With the encouragement of the deeply faithful Prince Shôtoku, the new religion struck its roots deep and brought a new face to Japanese art. Its pervasive influence is to be seen in temples such as the Hôryû-ji, in statues, miniature shrines, banners, and numerous artifacts, and the sense of form already brought to a considerable level of development in the archaic age underwent a change in its confrontation with new methods and simple yet dignified new modes of expression. Buddhist art includes Grecian elements transmitted through China and Korea, the vine pattern so popular in Buddhist decoration being a good example. In the succeeeding Nara Period, the Asuka styles were assimilated and softened. Buddhism was still more active, under the protection of the now firmly established central regime. The flourishing culture of T'ang China, with which intercourse had been established, was promptly transmitted to Nara, and Buddhist art reached a climax of grandeur and splendor. The murals of the Hôryû-ji, which were unfortunately lost a few years ago, and which contained Indian elements; the great Roshana of the Tôdai-ji in Nara; and the delicate handicraft objects preserved in the Shôsô-in storehouse—in all of these are to be seen most clearly the elements of an approach to beauty that spread over the whole of Asia in this remarkable period.

From the point of view of Japanese art, however, Asuka and Nara were periods of new development under stimulus from the continent, and in a sense periods of energetic acceptance of foreign influences. It was rather in the succeeding Heian Period that these influences were wholly assimilated to the indigenous Japanese aesthetic sense, and made to bring forth new fruit. In and after this period, the capital city was Kyoto, and the character of the culture too changed from the grand extroversion of Nara to a softer and more composed introversion. The esoteric Buddhist sects were introduced by Saichô and Kûkai. Dusky mountain fastnesses like Mt. Kôya and Mt. Hiei became the sacred places of esoteric Buddhism, and there the art of the esoteric sects was given profound expression.

In the late Heian Period, when commerce with T'ang China was cut off and the security of life under the Fujiwara aristocracy continued, the foreign influence became weaker, and a soft, lyrical Japanese manner was perfected. Yamato-e or "Japanese painting" took the place of T'ang painting, Chinese characters gave way to the *hiragana* syllabary; and the two, *hiragana* and the Yamato-e, were combined in the picture scroll to produce such masterpieces as the Genji Scroll and the Shigisan Engi Scroll. The Jôdo or Pure Land Sect, a simplified Buddhism, was founded to serve the religious needs of the masses, and new art forms developed to express the sweetness of the Pure Land. Soft, round Buddhist statues in the style of Jôchô, and paintings of the "welcoming" Amida to answer to the highly cultivated life of the aristocracy, display in one of its classical forms the elegance and delicacy of Japanese art. One is justified in feeling that the Buddhist spirit melted into a certain aesthetic sense of the ephemeral and evanescent to give birth to new beauty. Buddhist art had become remarkably Japanized, and upon the archaic Japanese base it brought forth Japanese fruit. In the succeeding Kamakura Period, the culture of the Fujiwara aristocracy was inherited by the military clans, who made an attempt on the other hand to return to something simple and powerful. For a time there was new vigor, but from the thirteenth century a decline set in and artistic energy waned. In this classical era, the era of Buddhist art, a distinctive style was perfected from the late Heian Period on into the Kamakura Period, and the elegant feeling for color and decoration that thus matured, as well as the lyrical and rhythmical emphasis on line drawing, gave new depth to the peculiar characteristics of archaic art, and, with increased softness and harmony, brought into focus one aspect of Japanese beauty—the source of the Japanese sense of beauty ever since. It should not be strange that its influence has continued uninterrupted down to the present.

III: If in the classical periods the softness and the lyrical harmony of archaic art were given variety and depth and a general elegance, the third or near-modern era brought a self-realization which led to a new development in archaic art, in its simplicity and plain strength and modesty. A new tendency accompanying the Japanization of Zen Buddhism became the axle upon which the advance was made. It is said that since the appearance of the simple ink washes of Sung China the art of Asia has been moving at right angles to the art of Europe, and as a matter of fact in Japan too there developed an art considerably different from the realism of Europe. The Muromachi Period was, like the Kamakura Period before it, an age of military dictatorship. Art, however, was no longer the servant of religion. The teachings of the newly risen Zen sect placed primary emphasis on self-realization, and in the art that came with it from Sung and Yüan China, the goal was in most cases not worship but appreciation. The ink wash developed from this starting point, and, though at first it reflected the landscape of China, it presently was put to the uses of an extreme Japanese expressionism at the hands of such masters as Sesshû and Kanô Motonobu. While embracing the lyrical softness so characteristic of the Japanese race, they set about achieving a sharply intuitive manner of expression, and gave an aggressive push to the simplicity and terseness inherited from archaic times. This artistic attitude also penetrated the tea ceremony, the Nô drama, flower arranging, and linked verse, to become the basis of all the arts of near-modern Japan.

It led at a stroke to the brilliant successes of the Momoyama Period, a period ushered in politically by Oda Nobunaga and Toyotomi Hideyoshi. The Momoyama Period shows at its boldest and most splendid what is fundamentally Japanese in art. By now quite liberated from the old religions, art was made to breathe the fresh life of the people. Painting, the handicrafts, and architecture all reached new heights, and numerous masters, beginning with Sen Rikyû in the tea ceremony, Sôtatsu in painting, and Kôetsu in the handicrafts, rode in upon the new tide. It should also be noted that Spanish and Portuguese appeared in the Momoyama Period, bringing Japan too under the influence of that universal wave, the Renaissance.

The powerful national art of the Momoyama Period gradually declined under the Edo Shogunate. Particularly with the imposition of the exclusion policy, interest became involuted and in the end focussed on miniature forms. There were tendencies of considerable importance, such as the art of Kôrin, successor to the school of Kôetsu and Sôtatsu, the realism of the Maruyama school in response to the modern spirit of rationalism, the development of the Ukiyo-e with the rise of a popular demand, and the Nanga school based on the free spirit of men of letters. On the whole, however, the period was not able to escape its narrow bounds, and produced no aggressive art comparable to that of the preceding period. Thus Japanese art with its two great traditions, the lyricism of the classical periods based on a sense of evanescence, and the intuitive expressionism of the near-modern periods, collided with the culture of the Occident. With the Meiji Restoration of 1868, we enter the modern period.

IV: Art in Japan in and since the Meiji Period has developed in the clashing and mingling of the tradition handed down from classical and near-modern times on the one hand and, on the other, the Western art which spread with the growth of modern capitalism. Nihonga or "Japanese painting" has relied on traditional techniques and attempted to throw off its shell in response to new currents, while Yôga or "Western painting" has set about importing each new trend from the West. It cannot be denied, however, that neither of the two streams has fully realized itself, and that modern Japanese art may perhaps be summarized thus: the Nihonga has been in danger of becoming fossilized in its tradition, and the Yôga, in its confused and breathless imitation of the West, has been unable to establish an identity of its own. The special characteristics of Japanese art, the straightforward simplicity of the archaic ages, the decorative sense with its mood of evanescence in the classical period, and the vital, intuitive expressionism of the near-modern periods—the characteristics of this art are in the modern world becoming more and more abstract and mechanized. Modern Japanese art is in the midst of a struggle to discover how to live in such a world, and the struggle is in the final analysis a part of that great universal problem, the mating of the cultures of the East and the West. (*See Pls. 35~39*)

CONTEMPORARY ART IN JAPAN
by TAKACHIYO UEMURA

Modern art in Japan has followed a course basically different from that in the West. Even today in Japan there exists a school of traditional Japanese painting which has produced a number of great painters with a strong hold upon the domestic market. Modern art in Japan is not, however, the product of a modernization of this traditional Japanese painting; it developed out of the school of modern Western art, which has its roots in the impressionistic realism introduced to Japan from France in the middle of the Meiji Era, or the last two decades of the nineteenth century. An outstanding feature of the world of art in Japan is the fact that there are two separate fields: traditional Japanese painting, commonly known as "Nihon Ga", and modern Western painting, commonly known as "Yô Ga". When speaking of modern art in Japan, one usually refers to the latter only and excludes the former. The fundamental reason for this distinction is the fact that, in comparison to modern Western painting with its theory of formative art based upon the concepts of modern internationalism and individualism, traditional Japanese painting, though retaining its refined technique, unique and decorative beauty, and oriental, spiritual, and intuitive charm, was wanting in modern thought and feeling.

Though constituting separate fields, Western and Japanese painting either consciously or unconsciously influence each other. Japanese painting is being stimulated by Western painting, and the latter too is showing a bent *attributable* to the former. Thus the works of Ryuzaburô Uehara (*Pl. 40*) and Sôtarô Yasui (who died late last year), generally recognized as the two greatest masters in contemporary European-style painting, may be described as representative of the Japanese crystallization of impressionistic realism. Umehara studied under Renoir and perfected a unique style through the adaptation of an oriental sense of colour. Yasui, who studied under

Laurens, was greatly influenced by Cézanne, and his style is distinguished by its portrayal of Japanese landscapes in Cézanne-like compositions. These facts account for the admiration which the new generation has for these two masters. Since their art is a product of the fusion of Western and Japanese styles of painting, the accomplishment of such a fusion in a more up-to-date form becomes the fundamental problem for future Japanese art and indeed is one that confronts Japanese artists today.

Since the concepts of modern internationalism and individualism formed the basic philosophy of modern Western artists, ideological reasons brought the development of modern art in Japan to a standstill during the Pacific War, when the nation was dominated by militaristic nationalism. The attainment of a democratic society through the defeat of Japanese militarism had its effect in a revitalization of modern art in Japan and subsequently led to further modernization.

A brief description of the art world immediately prior to the war should here be pertinent. Artists who stemmed from the impressionistic realism introduced from France had in the earlier part of the Taishô Era (1912–26) formed a group called the Bunten Circle, from an annual government-sponsored art exhibition of that name. The group compromised with and later conspired with bureaucratic forces in Japanese society; even now, it retains real power as a citadel of academicism. The process of the modernization of Japanese art, therefore, developed as a movement of resistance to and reform of the school of realism that had united itself with the government. The group that formed the core of this movement was the Nika Kai, which seceded from the Bunten Circle in 1914. One of its leading members was Tsuguji Fujita, the most famous internationally among Japanese artists. The Nika Kai was characterized by a vigorous internationalism and, while actively adopting the style of the School of Paris, it enrolled as its overseas members such artists as Yasuo Kuniyoshi, who was then active in the United States, and O. Zadkine, the contemporary French sculptor. In the matter of style it was responsible for introducing and developing Fauvism and Cubism. In 1922–23, towards the latter part of the Taishô Era, the internationalism of the Nika Kai was affected by a reactionary nationalism which attempted to reassess the values of traditional Japanese painting. This brought about a movement to secede from the group, and the Shunyô Kai (Kazumasa Nakagawa, Ryûsei Kishida, Shikano-suke Oka, Shôhachi Kimura and others) and the Kokuga Kai (Ryûzaburô Umehara, Kenkichi Tomimoto, Kôtarô Takamura, Bernard Leach and others) were born as schools advocating the tempering of the Western with the traditional. The movement was highly significant, since it was a conscious convergence of Japanese and Western painting. On the other hand, Katsuzô Satomi, who had studied under Vlaminck in France, and Takashi Nakayama, Zenzaburô Kojima, and Yatarô Noguchi, who had all been influenced by Derain, supported internationalism and formed the Dokuritsu Bijutsu Kyôkai, a body dedicated to Fauvism. The Nika Kai, however, still continued to be the stronghold of internationalism.

As art societies in opposition to the government-sponsored Bunten, the above-mentioned groups were to carry on the work of modernizing Japanese

55

art. After 1935, however, the forward movement of Japanese art came to an end, and non-governmental art societies lost their progressiveness. This was due to reaction and the rise of intolerant nationalism on the one hand, and to the stagnation of artistic doctrines on the other.

European art, led by the French, was in the era of Picasso and Braque, the era of avant-garde art, which was strongly internationlistic and which centered around abstract art and surrealism. Artists who had studied in France began to introduce this new movement to Japan from about 1937 and 1938, and the Jiyû Bijutsuka Kyôkei (Saburô Hasegawa, Masanari Murai and other), which emphasized abstract art, and the Bijutsu Bunka (Ichirô Fukuzawa and others), which advocated surrealism, were formed. At about the same time, a similar avant-garde group led by Tsuguji Fujita and Seiji Tôgô was born within the Nika Kai. These bodies constituted the camp of artists who, immediately before the war, once again supported the concepts of modern internationalism and individualism. The period, however, coincided with the so-called China Incident and, later, the Pacific War. Internationalism was disliked by the authorities, and, in the face of military oppression, the Nika Kai was forced to dissolve, while the artists belonging to the other two societies had to discontinue their activities entirely. Such then was the general picture just before the war.

Naturally the start of democracy and the revival of internationalism which followed Japan's defeat brought an important change in the world of art. Under the American Occupation, the government-sponsored Bunten was changed to the Nitten (Japan Art Exhibition), which in form is privately operated. Though this development meant in theory that government-sponsored exhibitions no longer existed, government influence, though weakened, continues to make its impact felt. A more important change, however, was the great reduction in the influence exerted by the Nitten upon the newer generation of artists. Furthermore, the fact that the younger generation is decisively giving its support to the modernization of Japanese art is of major significance, and shows the revival and growth of modern democracy and internationalism as the main stream of Japanese art. The artists who belonged to the Nika Kai, the Jiyû Bijutsuka Kyôkai, and the Bijutsu Bunka Kyôkai and whose activities were cut short by the war came to the fore in the postwar period and speedily increased their influence. The formation in 1946 of the Japan Avant-Garde Club by these artists was symbolic of the trend. The rapid development of international artistic interchange after the war should be mentioned as another important influence. It has taken many forms: the revival and increase of visits to Europe and the United States by artists and art critics; the holding of a Matisse Exhibition, a Picasso Exhibition, a Braque Exhibition, a Rouault Exhibition, and an International Art Exhibition in Japan; and the participation by Japanese artists in international art exhibitions in Italy, the United States, Brazil, Britain, etc.

In addition to facilitating the modernization of Japanese art, the developments in international artistic interchange contributed to the birth of a new reflective attitude which aimed at establishing a national individuality in Japanese art.

This is the subject which today confronts Japanese art and awaits exploration. It indicates the change in modern Japanese art from the stage of importing Western art to that of proceeding towards original creation on the basis of internationalism. In this sense, modern Japanese art may be said to be on the threshold of the most important period in its history. Today the trend towards the creation and establishment of internationally acceptable art which is yet peculiarly Japanese transcends the bounds of schools and art societies. Critical standards are also being oriented in this direction.

It should be appropriate here to introduce some of the more outstanding artists who are recognized as representative of Japanese art today. These artists, regardless of differences in style, have a common denominator in the fact that they all aim at achieving a form of artistic expression which combines modern formative techniques and products of the West with the traditions of Japan.

The advantage of a realistic approach is that full play can be given to oriental characteristics in line drawing, and comparatively many of the Fauvist painters have managed to produce a Japanese crystallization of their art. A number of the most distinguished painters are, therefore, to be found in this group. Among them, Takeshi Hayashi (*Pl. 41*) is a representative example. It is fascinating to see how, by using highly symbolic lines and colors, he manages to combine a modern sense of beauty with oriental tradition in his landscapes and figures.

In the works of Yatarô Noguchi and Tatsushirô Takabatake, the emphasis is on physical technique rather than on mental attitude; through their supple handling of the brush they manage to capture objects in a peculiarly light Japanese mood. Zenzaburô Kojima has displayed talent and originality by applying the composition of oil paintings to Japanese decorativeness. Shikanosuke Oka and Kinosuke Ebihara (*Pl. 43*) have a high reputation as artists who have given form to the poetry of Japanese life through the use of realistic techniques. Oka was influenced by Rousseau, and, using the technique of pointillisme, he produces beautiful and painstaking renditions of flower-baskets and imaginary landscapes and thus conveys the delicate sensibility and poetic emotions of the Japanese. Ebihara's forte is the use of sharp and exquisite designs as media for portraying the poetry of the masses. All the above-mentioned artists are in their fifties and studied in France during the era of the School of Paris. Among the somewhat younger group of artists with similar tendencies should be included Kaoru Yamaguchi, who participated in the Salon de Mai in Paris a few years ago, and Kazu Wakita, whose work was displayed at the Biennale Exhibition at Venice last year and who this year won the internal highest Prize in the international art competition sponsored by the Juggenhein Foundation.

The obvious leader of the visionary painters is Ichirô Fukuzawa, for he was the pioneer in bringing surrealism to Japan. He has held one-man shows in Paris and Mexico in recent years, and has exhibited in São Paulo. He won the Grand Prize last year at the International Art Exhibition in Tokyo sponsored by the Mainichi-Shimbun. His work features a combination of a sombre oriental sense of colour and a Western power of composition.

He will represent Japan at the Biennale Exhibiton at Venice again next year. Tarô Okamoto, whose works were displayed at the Biennale Exhibition at Venice in 1954, was member of the "Abstraction-Creation" group in Paris before the war, but he now shows a leaning towards surrealism. He is noted for his unique cartoon-like satirical abstractions. Among women painters, Yukiko Katsura, now resident in Paris, is recognized as an artist assured of a future, for she gives form to Zen-like themes in paintings endowed with humour and feminine decorativeness.

To take a glance next at the proponents of abstract art, quite a number of them are exploring the possibilities of expressing Japanese moods and feelings through purely abstract forms. Nagao Yamaguchi, a participant at the Biennale Exhibition at Venice in 1956, Masanari Murai, Saburô Hasegawa, who recently died in the United States, Tatsuki Nambata, Seijô Yamaguchi, Tatsuo Arai, who died soon after his return from Europe and America two years ago, Kigai Kawaguchi, Shigejirô Sano, and Minoru Kawabata are within this group. Since the interest of the younger generation of painters is at present concentrated upon abstract and visionary trends, these fields are the most active and, at the same time, the more complicated. Many of the artists who exhibited in the Young Asian Artists' Competition, including Jōsaku Maeda (*Color Pl. 4*), who won the grand prize and a number of other prizewinners, show marked tendencies in this direction. The attempts on the part of younger painters to deal with themes social in nature by abstract forms of expression should also be mentioned.

Finally, a recent development worthy of notice is the appearance of a group of painters in the traditional Japanese style who are trying to approach modern forms. A distinctive woodcut artist in this group is Shikô Munakata, who won the grand prize at the Biennale Exhibition at Venice. The emergence among calligraphers of a movement to combine painting and calligraphy, known as avant-garde calligraphy, and the dominance of abstract sculpture also deserve mention. Representative of the abstract sculptors is Shigeru Ueki, a participant in the Biennale Exhibition at Venice in 1956. His wood-carvings quite clearly portray Japanese moods and feelings in abstract form. Recent developments in calligraphy and sculpture stimulated a new movement in the art of flower arrangement. Several leaders of schools of flower arrangement, among them Sôfû Teshigawara and Houn Obara, are trying to create abstract and surrealistic space-objects based on the space-sense of flower arrangement. Tapié who is the leader of the Informal School and who was recently in Japan, found great originality in Sôfû's work. Of course such movements are still at the stage of experimentation, but there is no doubt that they will make valuable contribution to the task of establishing a national individuality.

Note:

This is a revision of an article which appeared in the magazine United Asia, June, 1954.

ART TODAY IN PAKISTAN
by JALALUDDIN AHMED

Art in Pakistan today is in a flux; by its very nature it is a crisis art, breathing fresh air brought from all sides, and representing a period of transition from what is to what could be, from the known to the unknown, both in theme and technique. The eternal conflict between the old and the new, the traditional and the modern, the accepted and the experimental, exists here probably in a more accentuated form than in many other countries which have, through the passage of time and crystallization of ideas, succeeded in striking some kind of a balance between the two.

For one thing, Pakistan is a young country, in the sense that seven years ago no Atlas bore this name, no Art carried that geographical label. On the other hand, paradoxical though it may seem, Pakistan is heir to a long-established tradition of art, comprising fine specimens of miniature painting and exquisite book illustrations executed by indigenous artists of the Mughal School, during the sixteenth and subsequent centuries, in the northern and western regions of the Indo-Pakistan subcontinent, including the areas which today constitute Pakistan.

The Mughal tradition has deeply influenced the *elder* generation of Pakistani artists, all of them born in the nineteenth century, and still practising in traditional methods or gone into comparative retirement now. Theirs is a serene, stable art governed by inflexible formulae, executed with meticulous, almost mathematical precision. Prolific in their output, technically correct in every detail and matured in unmistakable individual styles, they speak of a glorious past which impresses but somehow does not satisfy the young practitioner of art in Pakistan today, who ardently seeks fresh avenues for fuller self-expression through new techniques and newer themes.

That is the essence of the conflict which strikes the onlooker as he passes from Chughtai's classical ideal of the beauty of form to the 'down-to-dust' famine sketches of Zainul Abedin, from the perfect representations of Allah Bux to the completely non-representational art of Shakir Ali, from the astute draughtsmanship of Fyzee Rahamin to the raw but bold and stirring strokes of Ajmal Husain, from the elegant portraits of Askari to the abstractionist paintings of Zubeida Agha. Who indeed can predict the shape of things to come in the art of Pakistan a decade hence?

But of course we can talk of today in the context of yesterday: we can analyze the currents and cross currents as they have moved and shaped the individual styles such as we find them today, both among the elder generation of painters and the younger. Indeed one of the most gratifying results of the cultural renaissance in Pakistan has been the broadening of outlook which came in its wake, and which generally welcomed the artistic achievements of the west as a suitable basis for experimentation in the light of our own conditions. Though the individuality of the artist has found full play in subjects and media which are specifically drawn from the soil, the Western art movements have been subjected to a careful study and open-heartedly debated and accepted whenever found interesting enough. Of course, this applies to the younger generation more specifically than to the old. The towering personality of masters like Chughtai in contemporary Pakistani art derives as much from age and experience as from inherent artistic talent and calibre.

As already pointed out, the Mughal tradition has exercised very great influence on the elder generation of Pakistani artists, though in a different way in each individual case. The sheer opulence and brilliance of this tradition inspired them to paint their way into that august company of Mughal painters. That treasure-house of our classical art represents a remarkable gallery of pictures of contemporary life—Emperors and their courtiers, in palaces and on battlefields, freeing captives and hunting deer, visiting saints and listening to music—as well as realistic studies of birds and trees, and imaginative rendering of many romantic themes.

These last dominate the work of Abdur Rahman Chughtai, undoubtedly the finest living exponent of this school, and a brilliant water-colourist in his own right. A direct descendent of a reputed family of Mughal artists and architects, Chughtai started painting in the traditional style, but developed his own distinctive way of drawing figures and applying colours which bear the mark of a great personality. His first major work was the illustrations prepared by him for a new edition of the verses of *Ghalib*, a nineteenth century Urdu poet. (One of his illustrations, entitled *The Flame of Love* is reproduced here in colour.) He has painted extensively since and has produced more than a thousand paintings, etchings and outline drawings, remarkable for the liquid, flowing line of his graceful figures. In the early thirties, Chughtai visited Europe and, while there, became greatly interested in etching, a medium which he has since used with great vigour and felicity.

Commenting on his work then, an article in THE STUDIO pointed out that Chughtai's work is not merely influenced by Persian and Mughal painting of the past, but is 'an avowed rebirth of that art, with some recognition of modern progress and the stamp of individual genius'. In the intervening years Chughtai has perfected this individual style and he is today looked upon as an acknowledged master and as the builder of an impressive tradition. His style, however, has found few followers among the younger generation of Pakistani artists.

Allah Bux is another senior artist, steeped in traditionalism, though of a different kind. There is a mystic element in his work which reflects the mood and temperament of that 'artist-recluse', colourful and soulful. A great admirer of the Mughal tradition, he has not used the technique but only drawn upon the spirit inherent in it. This he has wedded to indigenous themes and imparted to it an unmistakable local colour. His treatment of legends and legendary subjects, and the mystic rendering of rocks, rivulets and tree-forms gives a descriptive and illustrative quality to his work which often tends to subordinate the technique to the subject. Like Chughtai, Allah Bux had no strict schooling in art, and learned it the hard way, on his own. At the age of sixty he still prefers to work non-stop in the studio on his paintings, without bothering himself too much about the outside world. The changing trends in art do not interest him. 'I paint what is in me', he says modestly but firmly, and he means it.

In sharp contrast is the career of S. H. Askari, who only a few years ago retired as the vice-principal of an art school. Askari is essentially a portrait painter and his portait gallery is filled with high personages obviously depicted with an eye on elegance rather than characterization. His technique is entirely Western, except that he shows his Oriental temperament in his endeavours to delineate even the minute details of his subjects such as jewellery or embroidery. Bright, scintillating colours seem to vie with each other on his palette, and he uses them with typical Oriental extravagance. He has also painted landscapes and historical scenes, but as one of his discerning critics has pointed out 'the intrinsic aesthetic significance of form receives little attention in his work while structural qualities and spatial relations are given secondary place to the exploitation of charms of surface texture, whether of human skin or stuffs'.

Among this group of painters, Fyzee Rahamin is perhaps the only one who has had a thorough grounding in Western methods of painting, and that too at the Royal Academy of Arts, London. He stayed in England and on the continent for a considerable time, painting portraits in the classical style and preparing himself for the brilliant career which lay ahead of him. It is very interesting indeed that an artist like Fyzee Rahamin, so thoroughly permeated in Western traditions both in technique and temperament, gradually came under the spell of the Mughal tradition, and went to it again and again for inspiration. Today, Fyzee Rahamin is not very active as a painter and is busy building up a museum and art gallery where his own and other paintings can be housed. A sympathetic guide and teacher to the young practitioners of art who throng round him, he often tells them that the way to be a good artist is simple. 'Be sincere and never be afraid to learn'. And that is where the younger generation begins.

Zainul Abedin, whose powerful sketches reminded Dr. Reiser of Goya's etchings, is a typical representative of the younger generation of artists in Pakistan who are restless, fond of experimentation, sincere and never afraid to learn. Those who admired Zainul Abedin two years ago for his intense realism may be surprised to know that he is going abstract. But he sincerely follows the call of the spirit irrespective of all extraneous considerations. He brings an open mind to bear on all problems of technique and expression. As Principal of the Dacca School of Art in East Pakistan, he has collected round himself half a dozen enthusiastic artists who are experimenting in various media: woodcuts, lithographs, aquatint and drypoint, besides water-colours and oils. Zainul Abedin himself prefers water-colour, which is his favourite medium, and his earlier landscapes bear eloquent testimony to his grasp over colour composition. But his recent experiments in etching and lithographs demonstrate how powerful his line can be.

Zainul Abedin is a fast painter, and revels in quick, bold strokes, remarkable for their economy and strength. This is true not only of his famine sketches but also of his recent 'Bull' studies, and his lithographs like *The Maiden* which are steeped in sheer luxury of form. Already in his moving water-colour, *Way to Quaid's Grave*, five years ago, he had indicated the direction of his future career, and his increasing interest in etching as a medium and abstractionism as a technique is easily traceable to the early lessons in realism learnt when he first put a crayon on rough sheets of waste paper.

In the group working at Dacca with Zainul Abedin, Safiuddin is perhaps the most promising. Woodcut is his favourite medium and his *Way Through Jungle* is a beautiful work of design and composition. Safiuddin's primary interest lies in technique and his experiments cover a very wide field. Two other colleagues of Zainul Abedin are Anwarul Haque and Qamarul Hasan, both belonging to the Dacca School of Art. The former has chosen oils for his portraits and real-life scenes drawn from the lower and middle strata in East Pakistan, and the latter is experimenting in powerful outline drawings which certainly owe their inspiration to Zainul Abedin's famine sketches but have gone further in adapting that technique to more pleasant and delightful subjects.

The most vocal and prolific group among the younger generation, however, is that of abstractionist painters. This includes those who adopted the abstractionist technique from the very beginning, like Shakir Ali and Zubeida Agha, as well as those who began by painting in the traditional representational method, but are now attracted more and more towards abstract art and have adopted it as an experimental measure in their search for a new kind of realism: painters like S. M. Sultan, Ajmal Husain and even A. S. Nagi (*Color Pl. 5*). Indeed the word 'group' may have to be stretched beyond the accepted sense of the term, for these free experimenters have very little in common and are far apart from one another in outlook, approach and temperament.

Zubeida Agha is perhaps the most popular, for she was the first to introduce her abstract work at an exhibition, soon after the establishment of Pakistan. Shakir Ali is her senior, and his work is maturer, but it was through the exhibition of Zubeida Agha's paintings that an interest in this technique was aroused. Today Shakir Ali, who is also the Principal of the Mayo School of Art at Lahore, has attracted a number of very promising young painters like Haneef Ramay, A. J. Shemza, Pervez, and Safdar (*Pl. 45*), who have painted extensively in this technique and have found it quite congenial to their talent and taste. Shakir himself, now in his late thirties, is full of the enthusiasm of youth and is a patient, diligent worker, very modest and shy by temperament. Unlike Zubeida Agha, Shakir Ali has had strict academic training in art and is a meticulous draughtsman. He was introduced to abstract art during his extensive travels on the continent and it is the love of pure form which has given him a quite distinctive style.

Zubeida Agha has recently returned after a long stay at Beaux-Arts in Paris, and her earlier ideas about painting have undergone considerable change. Of course she has returned to abstract art almost with a vengeance, but she is not so utterly non-representational in her recent work as she was in some of her earlier paintings like *Beethoven's Fifth Symphony* and *Wisdom*.

S. M. Sultan, who now seems to have gone over completely to abstract art, began by painting landscape, his *forte* two years ago. The soft green and blue of his native East Pakistan inspired him to paint at an early age, though it was much later, during his ramblings in Kashmir and the Punjab, that he found time and opportunity to observe nature in all its glory and paint it. Today he talks lightly about his earlier work and revels with a child's delight in the play of colour and linear pattern which inspires his abstract studies of what he calls 'moods rendered in colour'.

Unlike Sultan, Ajmal Husain is not interested in 'moods', but in forms and figures full of life and action, struggling to come out of the canvas and 'to happen'. There is a rare freedom in his work which seems to throw all rules of draughtsmanship to the wind, but even his stray lines leap to life and become pregnant with deep, unexpressed feeling. He calls his style 'neo-realist', though actually what he is trying to do is to adapt the abstract idiom to representational work.

A. S. Nagi is a slow, but steady painter, concentrating on portraits. In fact he is one of the few practising portrait painters in Pakistan and though a year's stay in Paris has enticed him to abstract art, he is wise not to yield to that temptation, except very casually. He insists on realism in his portraits and has already achieved considerable success in this most difficult of all art forms. He is not prolific but his work is of a very high standard and his place in contemporary Pakistani art is quite secure.

A sculptor who occasionally also paints is Ozzirr Zuby. His primary interest is sculpture and even his paintings have a sculpturesque quality about them. He has accepted the abstractionist technique and it is yet to be seen what he can make of it.

Finally mention must be made of a promising young painter who is coming up: Ali Imam. He seems to have an eye for colour, and can compose a picture, two big assets to start on an artistic career. He is perhaps the youngest of them all and apparently has not had the opportunity to paint at leisure. His drawing is weak and he has yet a long way to travel before his future can be predicted as an imaginative landscapist. But given time and opportunity, he may grow into one of our finest water-colourists.

There are a number of artists in Pakistan today who have given up painting—in some cases only temporarily—for reasons not very difficult to guess in a country where opportunities for art as a profession are obviously limited. Some of them, like Dr. Salimuzzaman and Mohammad Husain (*Color Pl. 3*), had already made a name in pre-partition India and now prefer to rest on their laurels. Others, like Sheikh Ahmad and Nasir Shamsie, have been concentrating more and more on commercial art for which there is a very heavy demand. Sheikh Ahmed has lived for many years in the United States and has also taught for some time at the Central School of Arts in London. Some of his earlier portraits are remarkable, but he is a theorist rather than a devoted practitioner of art, and is at present busy illustrating books for American publishers. Nasir Shamsie, who began with the traditional method of painting in the Bengal style, later took to modern Western painting in water and oils. He draws from life or composes in the studio from memory. Lately he has been concentrating on commercial art and designing, but his interest in fine art continues and his eventual return to the fold can be easily anticipated.

PHILIPPINE ART
a brief history
by GREGORIO G. LIM

The Philippines being an Oriental country, one would naturally expect its culture and art to be oriental in character. That this is not the case is explained by the fact that for almost four hundred years the nation had closer ties with Spain and the United States than with any of its neighboring countries. Its peculiarity in Asia is that it is the only Christian nation, the third largest English-speaking nation, and the most westernized nation. It has, therefore, frequently been susceptible to the influences of western art and culture.

After the discovery of the Islands by Magellan in 1521, Spain ruled for more than three hundred years with the sole purpose of converting the people to the Christian faith. The Spanish conquistadores made the Filipinos forget everything Asian or Malayan in order that western ideas and customs could be easily assimilated, customs which were, of course, suitable to the Christian way of life. Their mode of writing, way of dressing, and family customs were changed. Their music and folk dances show the unmistakable influence of Spain, although the "Tinkling" dance is originally native. The "Kundiman" songs and most of the native dances represent a blend of the Malayan and the European, and these have a charm of their own. Showing varied executions, interpretations, and expressions of the blended form, they have become typically and distinctly Filipino. Recently, an operetta, "NOLI", was shown to the public and acclaimed a typically Filipino masterpiece. It is based on the famous novel by the greatest Filipino patriot, Dr. Jose Rizal.

Very little is known of Filipino art and culture Before 1521. Although the Chinese were already in contact with the natives before the Spaniards came, they left little mark except on certain family customs and word usages, and there is no trace of their influence on Filipino art. This is probably due to the fact that trading was the main purpose of their coming to the Islands. We may infer that Filipino art at this time was similar to the primitive art now surviving among the aborigines or mountain people of Northern Luzon (the Negritos, Igorrots and Ifugaos), and to that of the Moros or Mohammedans of the South (Mindanao). These primitive civilizations were untouched by the western colonizers due to the natural barriers protecting and isolating mountain peoples, and to the ability of the Moros to repel repeated Spanish invasions. They therefore retained their own culture unadulterated. In some of the country's household articles, apparels, weapons, and minor architectural carvings and ornaments, the Hindu, Indonesian, and Arabic or Moorish influences can be noticed today. The Mayan or Aztec (Mexican) influence is also present, brought by the galleon trade between Mexico and the Philippines during the Spanish period.

The art of the Igorrots or the Ifugaos that can be best appreciated is in their wood carvings of idols, human and animal figures, examples of primitive abstraction that surprise masters of modern art. The bodies, faces and extremities are distorted for solidity and balance of design. The lines and forms are very cubistic, with the omission of natural details. There is so much sense of rhythm and personal expression that every piece is very exciting art.

The art of the Moros is mainly Arabic because of their Islamic relations with the Arabian countries of the Middle East. It is purely geometric and symbolical and more decorative and elaborate in colors and designs. Their religion prohibits them from copying human and animal forms. Their art is to be found in metal inlay, textiles, boats, weapons, and architecture.

There is an important similarity in the arts of the Moros and the Ifugaos especially in the colors of the textiles and house decorations. The favorite colors are strong red, orange, yellow, and green. Usually two opposing colors are placed side by side to produce an effect called blinding or sour by foreign observers. But these are the colors of the tropics, and their use in Philippine art today has given a Filipino touch to the western style of painting, and thus distinguished it from its western counterpart.

Western artistic influence in the Philippines was first felt when religious institutions began to function as schools for art. The early paintings of the Filipinos were naturally religious. Church decoration was at first done by Chinese craftsmen under the supervision of priests. The Spaniards were appreciative of these Chinese, whom they called "Sangleys". Most of their works were sculptural in nature. Together with the missionaries they acted as tutors to the native artists. But the temperament of the Filipinos is better suited to the art of painting. At first most works were done in churches and on altars in the homes of the rich, who had ecclesiastical permits allowing artists to work outside the church. In 1785 King Charles III issued an order permitting painters to practise their profession without permits. From religious paintings they shifted to portraits, which came into great demand, especially among well-to-do families.

Damian Domingo, a native mestizo, is the earliest painter on record, and he has therefore been designated the first Filipino painter. Only two or three of his religious paintings, done on copper, survive today. The works of his contemporaries and earlier painters were probably destroyed. Climatic conditions are harmful to any painting medium, and glue was moreover popularly used as the vehicle for pigments at the time. Fresco painting was never practised. The first known art school was opened by Domingo in 1817 (or 1820) and it was so popular that the government became its patron. After his death the school was replaced by the Academia de Bellas Artes, established by the government with Cortina and Nieto, two Spanish painters, as heads of the faculty. Agustin Saez, another Spanish painter, succeeded them and was the first teacher of the greatest Filipino painter, Juan Luna y Novicio, who is also one of the country's patriots. Luna participated in our struggle for freedom against Spain. There were other painters in this period who gained much prominence, among them Lorenzo Guerrero, who succeeded Saez as teacher to Luna; Isidro Arcejo, D. Gomez, and the Asuncion brothers (Jose, Antonio, and Hilario). Especially notable was Antonio Malantic, whose surviving works show him to be a master in his own style, much influenced by European masters but with a perspective similar to that of Chinese art.

The opening of the Suez Canal in 1869 brought Europe much closer to the Philippines, and more European influence could therefore be expected. Styles among succeeding artists are distinctly European, a fact which has persisted to the present time. Paintings became more and more academic, with portraits, still-lifes and landscapes as common subjects. In the last half of the 19th century, Juan Luna and Felix Resurreccion Hidalgo are the names foremost in Philippine art. For many years they studied in Europe. Luna is the first Filipino to gain international recognition, winning a gold medal of the first class for his huge canvas, Spoliarium, in the Exposicion Nacional de Bellas Artes of Madrid, Spain, in 1884. This masterpiece is now in Museo del Prado and a copy by the same painter is in Moscow. Hidalgo was also a recipient of several awards in art expositions in Paris and Madrid. This accomplishment shows that a Filipino could be as able as any European masters.

The Philippine Revolution and the coming of the Americans in 1898, led to the temporary closing of the schools and universities. With the beginning of the 20th century, genre painting started to appear, more fully matured than when it first appeared before the time of Luna. Outstanding as a teacher, authority, and a genre painter was Fabian de la Rosa, who painted in the classic style with delicate finesse and modulated colors. Even his portraits and landscapes have the qualities of genre paintings. Most of the painters of his time had no formal schooling and de la Rosa's way of painting was, therefore, the fashion of the period.

The Escuela de Bellas Artes (School of Fine Arts) was finally revived in 1906 to become a part of the State University of the Philippines. Meanwhile, photo-engraving was introduced, and the illustrator's art began to assume an important place as an art by itself. The leading illustrator of the time was Jorge Pineda. Prominent painters were Rafael Enriquez, Miguel Zaragosa, Felipe Roxas, T. Sucgang and Joaquin Herrera. Since all of them were trained in Europe, they were well informed to revolutionary art in Europe, the impressionists and Cézanne. De la Rosa being the head of the

School of Fine Arts and having a controlling influence over local painters, however, impressionism did not get a foothold in the Philippines. He called the impressionists "not modernists but decadents". In the last of his canvases some believed that he finally adopted this method of painting, but others explained that the change of style was unintentional. It was caused by his failing eyesight.

During the early decades of the American occupation, painters continued to paint native life and surroundings. Pablo Amorsolo, Ramon Peralta, and Vincente Rivera y Mir made contributions in the development of genre painting. Foremost among this group was Fernando Amorsolo, the cousin and pupil of de la Rosa, who, after his studies in Paris and Madrid, succeeded the latter... No other painter, past or present, has so many admirers, imitators, and followers. His influence persists to this day, and his name has become not only a proverb in Philippine art but also a school by itself. He is looked upon now as a great master in the traditional field. His broad slashes of light and subtle gradation of sweet colors derived from the impressionists, and his mastery of forms and designs was something new. He became the idol of the local art world. He is known for his beautiful genre and native landscapes, and he is at his best in historical subjects and portraits. Buenaventura, Peralta, D. Castaneda, J. Pereira, and J. Pineda belong to the school of Amorsolo. Guillermo Tolentino, our foremost sculptor, belongs in this same period.

In 1928, Victorio Edades, an architect and painter who studied for several years in the United States, returned to become director of the School of Fine Arts of a private institution, the University of Sto. Tomas, the oldest school in the country (older than Harvard). In the following year he exhibited his Cézanne-like canvases and became the first to introduce modern art. But his style was thirty years behind the latest trends in Europe. Edades caused so much agitation and opposition in local art circles that artists became divided into two schools of thought, the academic school and the rebel modern group. Carlos Francisco (*Pl. 53*) and Galo Ocampo were the first to go to Edades. Francisco, who is more rural than any of his contemporaries and shuns city life, may be considered the greatest Filipino muralist. He paints in a native idiom the simple community life of provincial people. His style is Gauguin-like with exciting colors, flattened shapes, and rhythm and balance in delicate distortions. Ocampo (Galo) is a surrealist and now a stained-glass and mosaic artist. Another addition to this group was Diosdado Lorenzo, who arrived from Spain and Italy in 1936.

Just before World War II, another group of modernists came to the front. Their canvases showed more abstraction and went much farther than those of the Edades group. They were Vincente Manansala, who had just returned from studies in the United States, Canada, and Europe (*Color Pl. 6*); Hernando Ocampo, a writer turned painter; and the Chinese artist Donald Dan Ming. Cesar Legaspi, who joined them later, is noted for his semi-representational abstractions expressive of native feelings and sufferings. Manansala is now a painter to watch. His canvases, although very modern, show a typically Filipino instinct and consciousness. Three years ago, he won first prize at the International Spanish Biennial Exhibition. He also won the top award at the United Nations Art Contest, and second prize in the First Southeast Asia Art Conference and Competition, 1957. Hernando Ocampo is now a non-objective painter. He is noted for his unusual colors and for his original style.

The reaction of the public was meanwhile very hostile. Then came the three-year Japanese occupation, which brought the modern ferment to a standstill. After the liberation, freedom was again given to artists. Newer subjects, such as war atrocities and destruction, human sufferings, and other upheavals stimulated the imagination of artists who had been waiting for a chance to give vent to free native feelings. In the traditional field, Antonio Dumlao, a self-taught artist, Simon Saulog, Romeo Enriquez, Juvenal Sanso, Gabriel Custodio, and Demetrio Diego became prominent for their newer approach to native subjects and sentiments. Some of the minor artists were busy with the "souvenir" pictures which were in great demand from soldiers and tourists. The modernists, not caught sleeping, were also trying hard to gain public recognition. The "13 Moderns," later the "Neo-Realists," was a group formed by H. Ocampo, Legaspi, Manansala, Estella, Oteyza, and Demetrio Diego to hold occasional exhibits in modern trends still very much behind those current in the United States and Europe. The group disbanded because of a lack of general interest and support.

It is natural that a new movement must progress by slow and painful stages amidst the public's refusal to understand. But society, although indifferent at first, has to change with this changing world. We are living in a world different from the past. A new world means new ideas, thoughts, feelings, and expressions. Increased speed in transportation and communications is bringing us much closer to Europe and the United States. Numerous art scholarships have been granted by foreign countries to modern Filipino artists, and the Art Association of the Philippines has been formed and is making a great contribution to the development of art in this country. Modern art has therefore at length come of age. And the public has become responsive to this new experience in art. H. Ocampo, Manansala, Legaspi, the lady painter Magsaysay-Ho, Emilio Lopez, and Constancio Bernardo are very active avant-garde painters, widely accepted and admired. Newcomers who have won public recognition include Fernando Zobel, a non-objective abstractionist in the Western manner, Arturo Luz, Jose Joya, Romeo Tabuena, Ang Kio Kok, Hugo Yonzon, Lee Aguinaldo, and Manuel Rodriguez. Still experimenting in new media to suit their individual talents are Jesus Ayco, Rodriguez, Gregorio G. Lim, and Tomas Bernardo. Napoleon Abueva is a noted sculptor in the modern group.

The birth of the Art Association of the Philippines in February, 1948, was one of the most important events in the history of art in this country. It is the largest national organization of art lovers and artists conservative and modern. Most painters well known today first gained recognition through the activities of this organization. In the early years of its existence, under the untiring leadership of Mrs. Purita Kalaw-Ledesma, the association made the public fully conscious of the development and progress of art, and new trends appearing in the Philippines. It has been able to organize annually well-attended exhibits of both modern and conservative works; and it has sponsored almost monthly exhibitions of paintings offered by private companies like Shell and Stanvac, by UNESCO and UNAP, and by foreign legations and museums, and exhibitions by visiting and local artists. It conducts classes for both adults and children. The enrollment in these classes has trebled, making it necessary to conduct them almost the year around. Occasional cinema art forums have been organized. These activities are the most effective means of increasing popular understanding of art. Before the war, there was not even one art gallery; today there are many. It was through all these activities that the modern movement caught the eye of the public. Although the AAP, as this association is called, is a private civic organization, its advice has frequently been sought by the government, UNESCO, and foreign cultural agencies.

Perhaps the most important event in the Asian art world was the First Southeast Asia Art Conference and Competition held in Manila from April 27 to May 2 of this year (1957). It was sponsored by the Art Association of the Philippines under the presidency of Dr. Gregorio G. Lim. The participating countries were India, Malaya, Indonesia, Vietnam, Japan, China, Australia, and the Philippines, all represented by outstanding artists. It was the best festival of art ever seen in the Far East, judging from the comments of foreign guests. Delegates and observers discussed the history, trends, and progress of arts in their respective countries; the status and social position of the artist; and ways to promote closer relations between Asian artists. They made the conference permanent, with art exhibits to occur biennially, and the name was changed from Southeast Asia to Pan-Asia, to include all the countries of Asia.

To set in motion the decisions made at this SEA conference, Dr. Lim has almost completed preparations for a roving exhibition of the most advanced Philippine paintings and sculptures. The eighteen-month tour will touch all parts of Asia, Europe, and the United States.

Art exhibits are common not only in Manila but in provincial cities, such as Baugio Dagupan City, Pasig, Cebu, Iloilo, and Zamboanga. In these cities there are schools and private classes on art for both children and adults. The biggest schools giving degrees in fine arts are those of the University of the Philippines, a government institution, and the University of Sto. Tomas. All in all there are about seven hundred students enrolled in these art schools and classes.

ART IN SINGAPORE
by LEE SIOW MONG

For the purpose of this article, the subject will be confined to pictorial art. Anyone who knows Singapore and its peoples will have no difficulty in guessing the type of pictorial art that ought to flourish here. Singapore is mainly a Chinese city—about 80% of the population are Chinese—of the British Commonwealth, and a good showpiece among British Colonial territories. The Chinese bring with them their art and culture wherever they go and therefore one would expect a stronghold of Chinese pictorial art in Singapore. Because of the small percentage of Europeans in Singapore, one would not expect a strong influence of European pictorial art. But this is not the case. The Government has for a long time been a British colonial government, the official language has been and still is English, and the government educational system has also been English until recently. There has therefore been a high proportion of English educated persons among the population and western influence has been strong. The impact is felt in all spheres of life and pictorial art is one of them.

The people of Singapore were not outstandingly and publicly art conscious until about ten years ago. Before that, art exhibitions were rare and attracted very little attention unless the artist was of international fame. Some people were interested in art in their own ways, but there was little public attention. The children in the schools had their usual periods in art and the Education Department had an Art Superintendent. There was, however, little organized effort in pictorial art. This lack of interest is understandable because Singapore is a colony and a commercial post. Children went to schools mainly for economic reasons—to receive an education in order to earn a living. A very large proportion of the population consists of immigrants who came to do business and were either too busy or had no interest in art. But below the surface of this apparently barren cultural desert there were individuals and homes keenly interested in art. This was revealed not many years ago when art exhibitions became popular and frequent and collectors came forward to lend their collections for exhibition. But of course to be a collector of paintings is quite a different thing from being an artist; but this fact will show that the people of Singapore were not so uninterested in art as some people had been led to believe.

The post-war period in Singapore saw a sudden awakening in the arts, particularly in music and painting. The traditional Chinese scrolls and western oils or water colour are the main features of any art class or exhibition. Traditional Chinese painting, using mainly black Chinese ink to produce delicate shades, is fast giving way to more colourful expressions either in oils or water colour. The traditional Chinese hanging scroll still remains, although the painting itself is no longer traditionally Chinese. The quiet dreamy Chinese landscape with its characteristic effect of distance achieved by piling one object above the other so that the most distant object is at the top of the frame, is also getting rarer. Artists no longer sit in their studies and dream and paint impossible landscapes, but go out into the country or street corners with brush and canvas to paint what is in front of them. We have both impressionism and realism, and although there is no local artist yet who is anywhere near the international giants, one thing stands out very distinctly in the works of our local artists. The vigour of their lines and their fearless use of colours are characteristic of a growing nation building something new out of the best that has been brought from both the East and the West.

Perhaps. we can call this the experimental age of what may eventually be the art of Singapore or Malaya.

The various races that have emigrated and settled here provide innumerable colourful subjects for the artist. The perpetual sunshine makes it possible to go out with brush and canvas anytime anywhere. The swaying coconut palm has become a favourite subject not only for the convas but also for the Chinese hanging scroll. There is no lack of a crowd at an exhibition these days, but what is lacking is a proper gallery. Hitherto, exhibitions have been held at the Singapore Chinese Chamber of Commerce, a building of Chinese architectural design and rather suitable, and the British Council building, now being demolished to make way for a national library. Until a proper gallery is available, the lack of an exhibition hall is going to be very keenly felt. There is also no lack of organizations interested in the promotion of pictorial art, both Chinese and Western. There are now two academies of art and several voluntary organizations running art classes and occasionally holding art exhibitions. Most of the artists are imported, mainly Chinese. However, the enthusiasm during the last ten years will produce the artists we want in course of time. In my estimate, within another ten years pictorial art in Singapore will reach a new high level.

During this post-war period there has been an influx of artists, mainly Chinese, from Hongkong to hold exhibitions in Singapore. This has resulted in keen competition and consequently a rise in our own standards. Up to now all art activities have been voluntary, and the satisfactory results speak well for the efforts of voluntary organizations. Official sponsorship has been rare in the past, but it is expected that the new additional functions of the Ministry of Education next year in the field of fine arts and cultural relations should augur well for the arts in Singapore and other countries that are interested in our activities.

CONTEMPORARY THAI ART
by SILPA RHIRASRI

To write about modern Art in Thailand from an artist's point of view, that is to say, free from artifice, implies saying things which may be unpleasant to many people, but the faith we have in the talent of Thai artists forces us to be straightforward in our brief study.

People interested in Thai cuture, and particularly in Art, notice disinterest and absence of artistic judgment on the part of the Thai middle and upper classes. A second feature they notice is that many painters and sculptors, after reaching the age of about thirty, either abandon their art or carry it on without enthusiasm—these two things depriving contemporary artists of their artistic maturity and preventing them from reaping the harvest of their intelligence.

From these two observations one could imagine the Thai people not gifted in art—but such an idea is quite opposite to the real facts. Truly, the Thai have a remarkable artistic temperament. Their traditional art shows, in architecture, painting, sculpture and decoration, rare qualities. The old Thai had an extreme sensitivity in expressing meaningful lines, had a perfect judgment in planning their temples, had an exceptional capacity in modelling wonderful Buddha images, and had a peculiar sense of colours which, although bearing the character of eastern lightness, are always fine and harmonious. The ornaments in lacquer work, in metals, in inlaid mother-of-pearl, in cloth, etc., although always ruled by geometrical principles, are flamboyant, alive, reflecting the tropical vegetation eternally vibrating under the kiss of the wind or of the rain. Like Nature herself, these ornaments are the abode of a myriad of small creatures or are the background of religious or mythical figures.

In their folk art, from which we may judge the artistic temperament of a race, the Thai are fascinating. In studying art, Thai youths show themselves to be exceptionally gifted. Summing up, we may say that in art the Thai have a temperament similar to the Latin people of Europe. But as far as contemporary art is concerned, all these qualities seem to find no echo among the mass of the Thai. WHY? The answer lies in the old Thai culture; a sketchy panorama of it will help the reader to understand many things which could not be understood otherwise.

> 1st ......For what purpose was art made in the past?
> 2nd ......Who in the past was interested in or cultivated art as aesthetic expression?
> 3rd ......What was the Thai 'home' previous to modern influences?
> 4th ......What was the social standard of Thai artists in the past?
> 5th ......What are the possibilities of modernizing traditional art?

FIRST QUERY

Because of the social and political system, art in the past was done almost exclusively for religious purposes. Architects, painters, sculptors and decorators worked with utmost reverence and enthusiasm for those religious centres wherein the Thai people found their unique spiritual refuge for their present and future life. The king and a few of the highest nobles, having a refined taste, embellished their palaces with ornaments. They appreciated fine jewellery very much, fine metal work, fine clothes and all the small objects of applied art for common use.

SECOND QUERY

Art appreciation. There being no centres where aesthetic matters were discussed and imparted to young people, there could not be a popular 'conscious' appreciation of art. Only a few members of the royalty had the privilege of learning music, literature or other intellectual expressions. The population understood their conventional art 'subconsciously' and also as a medium by which they could see in plastic forms what they felt about their faith.

THIRD QUERY

The Home. One of the most important factors suggesting to people and almost imposing on them the embellishment of their homes with works of art is the architectural arrangement and lighting. So also is the habit of transmitting to future generations the paternal 'home' containing selected works of art, a fine library, etc. It is from these collections that a fine taste for beauty develops.

A glimpse at the past of Thailand shows the house to have been a comfortable resting-place, shaded from the glaring light of the outside. Its rooms were small, and the verandas with projecting eaves, so useful to keep out rain and sun, made the interior dark. In old times furniture was limited to a few pieces, or none at all: one bench-like bed, one very low, small dressing table, one case to keep trinkets, were all that a house possessed. Because in old times people squatted on the floor (a very comfortable habit for tropical countries) they had no use for chairs. Such an arrangement of the interior did not suggest collections of paintings or sculptures.

Accordingly, as we have already stated, the unique place where people could be in contact with art was the Wat. But this should not be thought of as a centre of the sort a gallery is for western people. The wonderful Buddha images, the fine mural paintings or architectural monuments were reminders of religious or legendary stories. If a Buddha image was a masterpiece or was only mediocre in expression, it did not alter the religious emotion of the beholder. It represented Buddha and that was what concerned the pious.

FOURTH QUERY

With reference to the standing of Thai artists in the old society, it was the same as that of a carpenter or a brick-layer or any other common workman. Such a state was not offensive to the class of artists, nor do we mean that in modern social life an artist is a 'superman'. An artist is a common man, but endowed with a super-sensitiveness which enables him to create, and, if backed by a comprehending society, artists may produce wonderful flowerings. The point is, however, that the old society was divided into upper and lower classes. Artists belonged to the latter class. This depressed condition lasted till a few years ago and still lingers in the minds of many people. A personal anecdote may enlighten the reader: When I arrived in Thailand, I shared my studio in the Fine Arts Department with two Thai sculptors. One day the Director-General came to see some works of mine: the two sculptors, in the presence of the director, who had the honorific title of Phya, squatted down on the floor bowing reverently in what to me seemed a servile manner. I felt ashamed and asked myself what an artist was held to be in Thailand. Since the day of this incident thirty-five years ago, Thailand has made enormous democratic progress. Young artists feel they deserve fairer treatment. The population has started to understand that an artist is a representative of the national culture. Still we suffer from what the Thai call 'Pu Yai and Pu Noi'—principals and subordinates. A higher general education of young Thai artists coupled with a proper understanding and evaluation of the intellectual values of the nation will soon eliminate even these small disharmonies inherited from the past.

FIFTH QUERY

With reference to traditional art in Thailand, there is not at present a real school carrying on the glory of the past. In general, present painting and sculpture in the old style is artistically so objectionable that we do not bother to classify it as art. It serves commercial purposes, sale to tourists, and it thus adds to the income of the country and nothing else. At present the production of ornamental and decorative works of art in Thai style is in the hands of Chinese artisans whose workmanship is cheaper than that of the Thai and more suitable for commercial purposes. Nobody can understand and execute Thai ornaments better than the Thai, but the buyer who cannot discern the good from the bad prefers the cheaper ones. Architecture in the Thai style has reached a crisis. Materials once used cannot be used nowadays because they would be too expensive and not as lasting as cement.

To think of rendering the finesse of ornament or other peculiarities of a wood structure in cement is an illusion. Modern Thai architects try to combine the old with modern ideas, but to my way of thinking, the result seems rather artificial. Thus Thai architecture is passing through the transitional period European architecture experienced about fifty years ago.

After many centuries, traditional art came almost to a standstill about seventy years ago. If no foreign influence had interfered with Thai culture, the old art, although already at the stage of creative exhaustion, would have gone on from its own momentum, but western civilization crept in, affecting Thai life profoundly.

Recriminations do not change facts. Like all other people, the Thai accepted modern civilization with its scientific and mechanical progress and comfort. The real fact is that the Thai at present enjoy a standard of living far superior to that of the past. In the realm of science and all modern appliances, the Thai are ready to appreciate every new discovery and apply it to their daily life. It is only in art that this people has remained traditional and traditionalism keeps them from appreciating modern expression. Accustomed to their conventional art, illustrating subjects well known from childhood, the Thai are at a loss to understand forms of art which they think imitations of foreign forms. Here, indeed, is a serious misunderstanding. Contrary to the western art of the 19th century, which represented for Thailand a foreign culture and was thus exotic for this country, modern art is universal and no race may claim its paternity. It may be adopted by every people without fear of imitating foreign expression. Modern art was born from scientific discoveries, from knowledge and education, and principally from the reciprocal influence of ideas and arts of all the races of the world. Asia and Europe, America, Africa and Australia, all these cultures fused together in creating the new artistic expression. There should be no prejudice against it, since it does not represent any particular race. Indeed, modern art has no national style; it is the individual expression of the artist, and it will surely impress his work with the peculiarities of his race. An Indian will always think as an Indian, a Thai as a Thai, an Italian as an Italian and so on. We may all speak the same language but the thought will always be individual. When we see an artist imitating a master it is because of lack of personality, or lack of capacity.

Some Thai and foreigners would like to see our artists blend modern with traditional art. The result would be a hybrid one. It is only in the spirit of old art that young artists may get inspiration, not in the form. For a clearer explanation of our theory let us review very briefly the character of traditional art and see what the modern artists could get from it.

TRADITIONAL STATUARY

In statuary a certain type of Buddha image was repeated for centuries. Some great Thai sculptors emerged now and then, creating statues which are the glory of the Thai genius. Mediocre followers, as usual, imitated those masterpieces without understanding them and produced a frigid, expressionless statuary.

Contrary to Java and Cambodia, the Thai, being followers of Hinayana

Buddhism, did not treat Jataka stories (describing the merits of the Buddha in previous lives) in bas-relief. Only after the 15th century were the Jataka stories represented in murals. The few bas-reliefs in stone or stucco or other material in Thai art do not approach the artistic heights of the Buddha images. Ornamental sculpture in wood or stucco was very fine indeed, but this belongs to ornamental art and does not help us in our brief study. In Thai traditional sculpture, therefore, only Buddha images can give inspiration to a modern artist.

TRADITIONAL PAINTING

The gesture and posture, costumes and jewellery of the divine or royal personages painted on walls or illustrating books on Buddhist cosmology derive directly from the classical theatre. Although extremely fine, this kind of painting cannot be considered a 'creation' because it is the reflection of another artistic expression. On the other hand, the figures representing common people are inspired by real life and show the old Thai painters at their best in observing the world. From this kind of painting a modern painter can get inspiration for decorative composition. I say decorative because what we call pure art is the result of some kind of emotion experienced by the artist from the world around him. Now the world depicted by old painters is 'past'. Modern Thai towns do not offer to our artists the sight of customs, scenes, manners of old. Modern civilization has remodelled everything and everybody's tastes. Landscape in traditional painting was treated very conventionally and has a dark background tonality behind the various groups of small human and animal figures or architectural masses. Thus there is no link here with the modern landscape. Portraiture or other paintings for decorating halls, etc. was not known in the past and there cannot be a connection between past and present here.

Naturally, we sympathize with those who would like to see contemporary art blended with traditional, but from this brief study of old Thai art, we can understand that it is so conventional, or represents a world so different from our own that the modern artist has no other alternative than to express himself according to his temperament and immediate surroundings. The change in art-expression was not sought after deliberately by modern Thai artists. It was one effect of modern life.

At the end of the 19th century Thailand adopted western civilization. Railways, schools, hospitals, roads, electricity, etc. shaped modern Thailand. After science and machinery, western art was introduced into this country. Royal and public buildings were designed in the western style and western paintings and sculptures were imported into Thailand from Europe. This meant the end of traditional art. Thai sculpture was not affected because, as we have said, it was limited only to statues of Buddha, but even sculpture was more and more commercialized. Thai painting, which, with its two-dimensional character and primitive perspective, reminds us of the painting of the Italian primitives, lost its fine qualities, in imitating the western three-dimensional landscape (while the figures remained two-dimensional) and introducing scientific perspective in the painted architectural structures.

For the same economic reasons the building of Wats came to an abrupt end. In old times the erection of temples was the highest ambition of Thai rulers and noblemen. In adopting modern civilization the national economy was turned to public welfare and the building of Wats was reduced almost to nothing. We have already stated that old Thai art was almost exclusively for religious purposes. Once the Wats were no longer being built, all other Thai arts lost their field of activity.

Such was the situation at the end of the 19th century. In the 20th century the trend towards the universal standards of the modern age was still more pronounced. Public and private buildings were erected in ferro-concrete, a material which changes the whole style of architecture. Modern costumes replaced the traditional ones. The army was mechanized; the house was furnished. The cinema and all other modern techniques were introduced. In a word, life in Bangkok became cosmopolitan. Till 1937 Thailand had European painters and sculptors working at the service of the king or for the governmental departments. Thai traditional painting was in full decline, though Thai sculptors still modelled their Buddha images in wax or stucco after old style or another.

Only in architecture were there able Thai artists, such as H. R. H. Prince Harisaranuwatiwongse and his pupil, Phra Prom Pichitr, who is still alive and with his pupils is still working in traditional Thai architecture at the Fine Arts Department.

A school of decorative arts (the Arts and Crafts School) existed in Bangkok for the purpose of keeping alive the old crafts, such as embossed metals, niello, wood and ivory carving, inlaid mother-of-pearl, etc. Some of the most gifted ex-students of this school applied themselves to commercial or semi-commercial painting with success, but no special college existed to train youths in the arts of painting or sculpture. It was in the year 1934 that the Fine Arts Department opened a School of Fine Arts for such a purpose. In 1938 Thailand had her first group of painters and sculptors to replace the European artists who till then had executed official works. The first group to graduate from the School of Fine Arts were employed as painters and sculptors at the Fine Arts Department and as art teachers.

Meanwhile, an energetic and able artist, Mr. Chit Buabus, on becoming the principal of the Arts and Crafts School, introduced modern methods of teaching, and thus raised the standard of artistic education.

Such was the situation twenty-five years ago. What could be done to revive Thai art? Was it possible to go back to old forms? No, because modern surroundings are quite different from those of the past. The writer, who is responsible for the organization of the School of Fine Arts (presently the University of Fine Arts) thought it would be logical to train young Thais, starting again from Nature—giving them a sound foundation in their arts. Of course, this meant an academic training, but, after all, we are convinced that this is the best method of training an artist. Once the young student has finished his art training he may express himself better in whatever style he likes because it becomes a personal matter and each artist has the right to express himself individually.

The reader should not think that we disregard the importance old art may have in modern expression. During their three years, the students have to do research on traditional old art, architecture, painting, sculpture and ornaments for three hours a week. This serves to stimulate in them a subconscious relationship with the spirit of the past, which is unchanging because it represents the essential peculiarity of the Thai race. Some Thai artists, such as Khien Yimsiri and Chalood Nimsameo (*Pl. 55*), have already been successful in creating works of art which, although very modern, bear the spirit of the Thai race. As everywhere else, few among the many students of art in Thailand are really gifted. The majority go into teaching, commercial work, or the government service. The best follow a two-year course of specialization (either painting or sculpture) after graduation.

Because in Bangkok there is no possibility of earning one's living as a professional artist, the best of the graduates are employed in the various official departments. For another two or, at the most, four years, these young artists work with enthusiasm and after this period the 'crisis' comes. They are just at the beginning of their careers, just at the time when an artist should work indefatigably to find his own personality. Stimulated by hope and example, the young artists make personal sacrifices to create works of art. They show these works at the exhibitions organized by the Fine Arts Department, by the Arts and Crafts School or by other groups of artists. Eventually their works are awarded medals and other prizes and so the hope of establishing themselves among Thai artists becomes a matter of fact. But their works remain unsold.

With rare exceptions, the rich, not being trained in art appreciation, do not embellish their homes with sculptures or paintings. The public buildings, gardens, etc. are not decorated with works of art. The result is that sculptures, which generally remain in plaster of Paris, fall to pieces while the paintings are presently lost. In Bangkok there is not yet a gallery of modern art and every work of art worthy to be preserved is doomed to be lost. Here lies the reason why Thai artists cannot reach artistic maturity. After their first success in the art exhibitions, after the period of enthusiasm, hope, and pride, depression follows, meaning the end of the young artist's activity. Some people say that the public lack of interest in art is due to the fact that Thai artists express themselves in a too modern way, but even when artists produce works in the traditional style, nobody buys them.

Of course, these regrettable conditions will change. New generations are more ambitious than the older ones. Higher education and wider knowledge of the intellectual values bound up with the culture of the nation, will bring, in two or three decades, a change after which modern Thai art will be affirmed. In the meantime, we watch a growing plant which will surely bear beautiful flowers. What gives us the certainty of the flowering of modern Thai art is the fact that some students are exceptionally talented. Every year we notice young Thais so gifted that our enthusiasm and hopes are renewed stronger than ever.

For the time being, practically all our hopes are followed by bitter disappointment because the cycle of development of every young artist is the same as that of his predecessors. But once art appreciation improves and Thailand is ready to accept free professional artists of standing, we know for a certainty that they will renew the glories of the past.

Artists such as Khien Yimsiri, Fua Haribhitak; Chalood Nimsameo (*Pl. 55*), Prasong Patamanuch (*Pl. 54*), Siddhidet Senghiran, Sawaeng Songmangmee, Chalerm Nakiraks, Sawat Tantisuk, Tawee Nandhakwang, Panom Suwanabhunya, Piman Moolpramuk, Chamras Kietikong, Paitoon Muangsomboon and many others are so much gifted that all of them could have reached an outstanding position. If Chalood Nimsameo, for instance, were working in the artistic ferment of Europe, or America, or Japan or India, he would become a very noteworthy artist. This young sculptor and engraver, a painter too, is now in Rome and Paris to see the old and modern art of Europe. He too is bound to accept the same routine government work, and by and by, of him too, I am afraid, there will remain only the bitter-sweet flavour of hope.

Young Thai artists as well as students of art understand and like modern art more than any other expression. This is quite as natural as it is natural for another Thai to prefer to drive a motorcar rather than ride an elephant. In general the style of Thai artists is realistic or impressionistic. They are at the beginning of their careers and impressionism or realism is the first stage which all modern artists have passed through. Others are quite personal and represent the object painted synthetically or by changing its forms according to the necessities of their conception. At the start, young painters have a rather dark tonality which after some years changes to brighter schemes.

No surrealism or abstractism is to be seen in Thailand. These kinds of art, if not treated 'childishly', as in fact they are in too many cases, require an intellectual maturity which our artists have not yet reached. In any case, to produce such art in Thailand would be out of place because our public has first to understand modern art in its simpler expressions.

What then is the aspiration of Thai artists? It is the same as everywhere—they want to express what they feel, not what others want. Is it wrong? Cannot the public understand that in our age art does not mean the faithful reproduction of the physical world? The camera, better than any human eye, may satisfy people who are so keen on realistic reproductions. But cameras cannot convey the 'invisible reality' of an object, a landscape or a living creature. Art renders these things with such power as no scientific means may render.

A classic Chinese painting depicting bamboo, or clouds and waves—a landscape or still life of Van Gogh are masterpieces not because they represent the visual world, but because they are imbued with the 'eternal spirit' of Nature. From Nature the artist receives an emotion engendering in him an abnormal spiritual, mental and muscular state. This abnormal 'state' enables the artist to create works of art emanating from the mysterious and mystic spirit of the 'invisible'. These facts cannot yet be understood by the Thai public and a modern artist who does not illustrate subjects related to public literary and religious knowledge is bound to be rejected as not conveying Thai expression.

To watch the visitors to art exhibitions is very instructive—many of them act as if they were expert critics of art. They do not know what personal sacrifices artists undergo to affirm Thai art as it deserves to be affirmed. Of course, both prejudicial criticism and disinterest on the part of those who should support art affect the morale of the artists. It is only when Thailand is requested to participate in foreign exhibitions or show to foreigners the activity of modern Thai artists that responsible people seem to be interested in the matter. But artists and their works cannot be produced by magic. It takes years to form an artist and years for him to produce valuable works of art. Those who really feel distressed at such circumstances are the few who see in art one of the greatest manifestations of our people's culture.

By pointing out the untactful criticism of non-expert people we do not mean that the public has not the right to criticize freely. What we resent is their 'prejudice' against modern expression, a prejudice which in many cases either conceals ignorance or excuses lack of support for art.

The public should understand that every artist tries his best to create something fine, but the majority of his works of art will not be worthy to be referred to as ART. This remark applies to modern art as it applies to the art of every people and every age. Greece, India, China, Japan, the Renaissance, produced a myriad of works but among this vast number, only a relative few have remained impregnable to the attacks of criticism and fashion. The rest have been lost, or represent productions good only for historical and archaeological records.

Accordingy, if in an exhibition of modern art, or among any other modern artistic productions, we find only some few pieces which give food for imagination and refine our feelings, then we should be satisfied and look at the lesser works as a necessary complement coming from where the good ones also emerge.

It would not be fair to conclude this brief study on Thai contemporary art without touching also upon some flaws on the part of our artists.

The majority of them do not cultivate sufficiently the general knowledge necessary for a modern artist. We have seen that at present art does not mean any more the illustration of religious or literary works. In the past a Thai sculptor modelling a Buddha image required only the support of his Faith. He had not to imagine peculiar conceptions. He had to feel and believe and if he was a genius he created a masterpiece which today still stands as such. A modern artist 'must conceive the subject by himself', must feel and must be capable of rendering it so convincingly as to have others experience his sensations too. Without knowledge a modern artist remains superficial. He is not able to transmit in his work the very spirit of things.

A second remark must refer to activity. With few exceptions, Thai artists are still under the spell of their blessed land which is so benevolent about their material needs. Life being easy, one is not stimulated to work 'hard'. But while this fact may be integrated into different branches of Thai activity, in art it cannot stand. Some are born artists, but even they may realize their promise only through indefatigable activity. Experience gives skill and skill is the counterpart of the natural gift.

Waiting too long for inspiration is a waste of precious time—very harmful to artists. To be a successful artist one needs a natural gift, enthusiasm and strength to bear serious sacrifices and suffering, for the life of an artist pivots around sacrifices and suffering. A man wanting nothing cannot create art.

COLOR PLATE

2 *Voice* (*Portion*)   by M. Husain, India

3 *Balinese Rural Scene*   by I. Reding, Indonesia

4 *Creation* by Josaku Maeda, Japan

5   *A Nude*   by A. S. Nagi, Pakistan

6 *"Give us this day"*   by Vincente S. Manansala, Philippines

PLATE

burma

7 *Wall Painting*   by U. Ba Kyi, Burma

8 *Landscape* by U. Ba Nyan, Burma

9 *Scene of Trivandrun*   by Mang Nla Aung, Burma

10 *Mother and Child* by George Keyt, Ceylon

11 *Design with Animals* by Chandramani, Ceylon

12 *Kandyan Dancers* by P. G. K. Fernando, Ceylon

13 *A Person*   by Ow Yang Wen Yuen, China

14 *A Woman and Chickens*   by Sha Yang, China

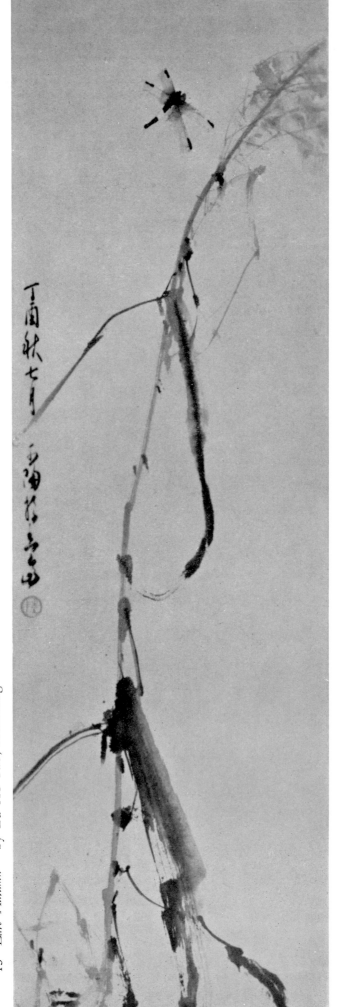

106

15 *Late Autumn*   by Lu Ko-Tao, Honkong

16 *Spring Landscape*   by Huang Lei-Sheng, Honkong

india

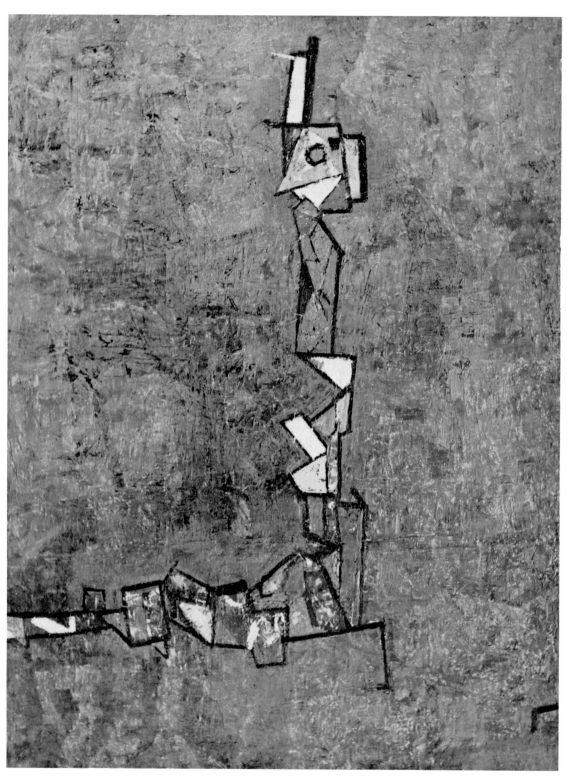

17 *Kites*   by M. Samant, India

18   *The Bird and an Egg*   by V. S. Gaitonde, India

19   *Three Figures*   by Ramchandra V. Savant, India

20 *A Dancer*   by Chavda, India

21 *Music*   by Profulla S. Joshi, India

22 *Winnowing*   by R. D. Raval, India

23 *Waterfall* by Amina Ahmed, India

24 *Prometheus* by Satish Gujral, India

25 *The Bereaved* by Ram Kumar, India

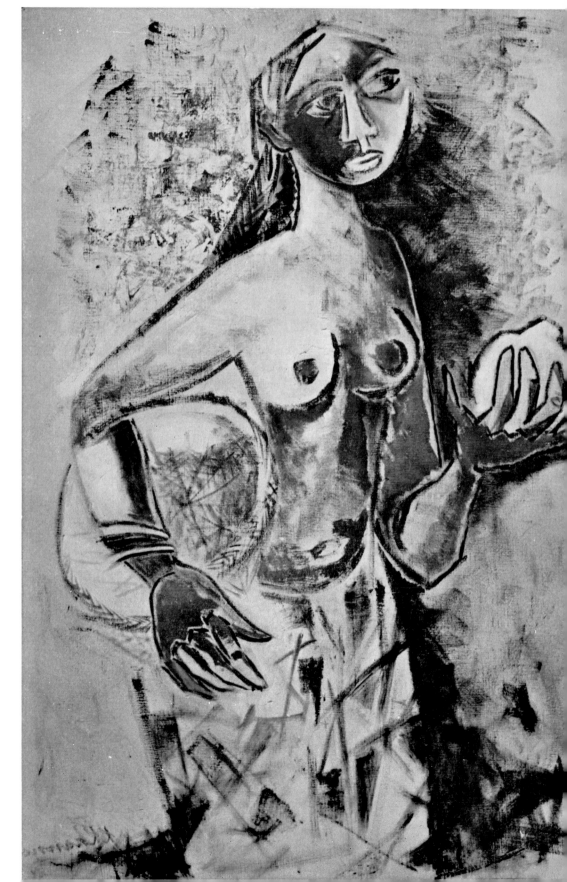

27 *My Mother*   by Affandi, Indonesia

28 *My Wife* by Agus Djaya, Indonesia

29 *Three Girls*   by Sholihin, Indonesia

30　*Ancient Life* (*Portion*)　by Widajat, Indonesia

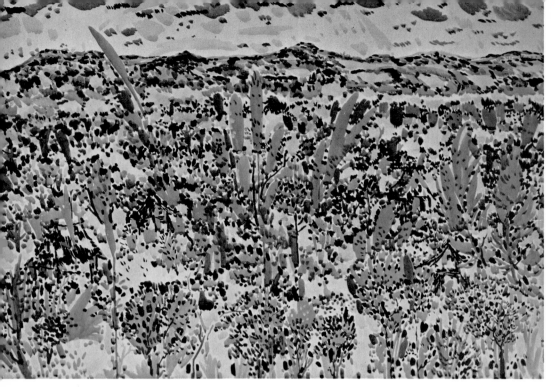

31 *Nature* by Mardian, Indonesia

32 *Landscape* by A. Wakidjan, Indonesia

33 *Bandung*   by Kartono Yudhokusumo, Indonesia

34 *Balinese Woman*   by But Mochtar, Indonesia

35 *Pink Plum Blossoms* by Seison Maeda, Japan

36 *Fault*   by Kyujin Yamamoto, Japan

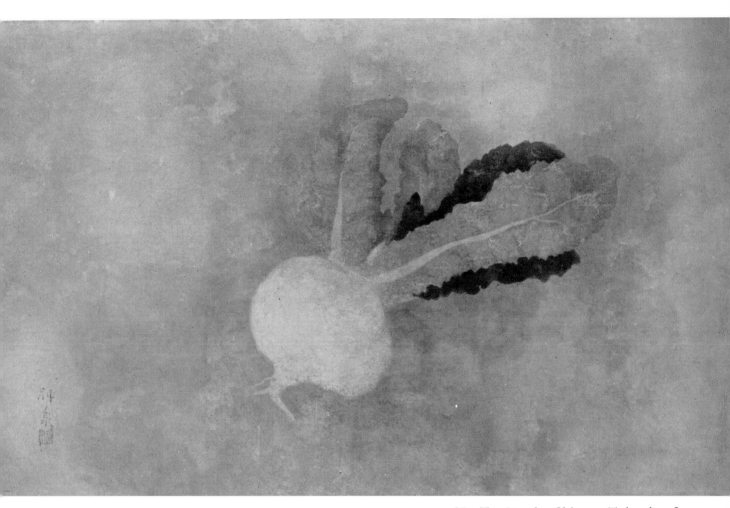

37 *Turnip* by Shinsen Tokuoka, Japan

38 *Blue Sun*   by Matazo Kayama, Japan

39 *Mother and Child*   by Hajin Iwasaki, Japan

40 *Mt. Fuji* by Ryuzaburo Umehara, Japan

41 *Woman in the Field* by Takeshi Hayashi, Japan

42 *Sculpture* by Seiji Chokai, Japan

43 *Shipwright* by Kinosuke Ebihara, Japan

44 *Traces of Blue* by Yoshishige Saito, Japan

45 *Birds* by S. Safdar, Pakistan

46 *Twilight*   by Mohammed Kibria, Pakistan

47 *Abounded*   by Syed Jahangir, Pakistan

48 *Gossip* by Abdul Baset, Pakistan

49 *Bali Maiden*   by Chen When-hsi, Singapore

50 *Singapore River* by Sim Kern Teck, Singapore

51 *Resting* by Leong Hong Ying, Singapore

the philippines

52 *Composition A*   by Emilians Ma Aclop, Philippines

53 *A Snack of the Workers of the Farm*   by Carlos V. Francisco, Philippines

54   *The Fiddler*   by Prasong Patmanuch, Thailand

55 *Morning Market*   by Chalood Nimsameo, Thailand

INDEX

144